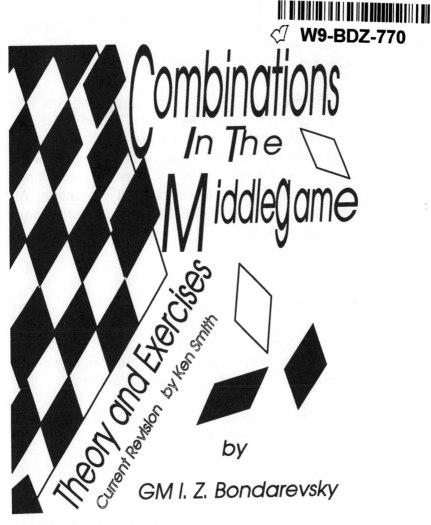

Combinations In The Middlegame

Theory and Exercises
Current Revision by Ken Smith

by

GM I. Z. Bondarevsky

Translated by Bernard Cafferty B.A., F.I.L. (Russ.)
Current revision examples by Ken Smith

1st Edition:
Printed and published by Chess (Sutton Coldfield) Ltd, England

2nd Revised Edition:
Printed and published by Chess Digest, Inc.

Authors: I.Z. Bondarevsky and revisions by Ken Smith
Editors: John Hall and Roy DeVault
Computer Typesetting: Roy DeVault
Cover: Elaine Smith
Proofreader: Roy DeVault and David Sewell
Final Preparation and diagrams: Roy DeVault
Publisher: Chess Digest, Inc®, 1601 Tantor (P.O. Box 59029) Dallas, Texas 75229

Send the publisher $2.00 for the New Chess Guide that catalogs every chess book for general sale in the United States. You are given publishers, page counts, notation and critical reviews. Also included is a free Chess Improvement course for beginners up through Master level players.

TABLE OF CONTENTS

The elements of combination - The sacrifice as the basic element of a combination - The definition of a combination- The calculation of a combination and the assessment of the final position - The genesis and logical nature of combinations.

Combinations based on attracting - Blocking combinations - Combinations based on diversion - Combinations based on square-freeing - Line-freeing combinations - Line closing combinations - Combinations based on isolation - Combinations based on destroying a guard - Combinations based on seizing a point - Destroying combinations - Combinations with blended motifs.

Translator's Preface

When the Soviet publishing house *Fizkultura i Sport* began publication of a series of chess books, I commented on their excellence, especially from a didactic point of view, though obviously for this purpose one needed a knowledge of Russian to be able to follow the text as well as the actual play in the examples quoted. I am pleased therefore to be able now to make one of these books available to the English-speaking chess public. As I also remarked in my review, the Soviet concept of a beginner is clearly wider than ours, and to make the book even wider in its scope and appeal I have added some supplementary material. I must confess that I have had some misgivings about the correct rendering of certain technical terms, but in the absence of an internationally accepted terminology each translator must take his own line on such matters. Also in translating certain extracts quoted from authors whose books are available in English I have followed the Russian text in those rare cases where it differs slightly from the English version. I trust that this book will give real pleasure to its readers and help those players who wish to learn to play combinations.

The Author

Igor Zakharovich Bondarevsky was born in 1913, learnt chess at the age of nine, but only began to play seriously in 1925, as a result (he says) of the interest created in the Soviet Union by the Moscow international tournament of that year. He first played in the Soviet championship in 1937, and in 1940 shared first place with Lilienthal in the very strong XII U.S.S.R. championship above Botvinnik, Keres, Smyslov, Boleslavsky,etc - this was undoubtedly his finest performance ever. In 1949 he was awarded the international grand master title. An engineer by training, Bondarevsky has played little in the last decade, devoting much of his time to organization, writing and training young players. His most notable success in this direction is the fine play of the former World Champion Boris Spassky, whose trainer Bondarevsky has been since 1961. Bondarevsky is on record as stating that he considers Capablanca the strongest player of the twentieth century, which is an unusual viewpoint for a Soviet player.

He has played in England only once - in the Hastings Congress of 1961-2 when he finished second to Gligoric.

B. Cafferty

Editor's Note

Be sure to set up each position on your chess board, even the simple ones. There is much to learn after each move. All examples after 1960 are current revisions by Ken Smith.

Dedicated to the late B. H. Wood, founder and publisher of "Chess", Sutton Coldfield, England.

The Basis of a Theory of Combinations

What is a chess combination? Naturally it is with the elucidation of this question that we must begin. However, a definition of what is called a combination is not such a simple matter as it might seem at first sight.

We will remark straightaway that chess theoreticians have defined the concept of a combination in different ways. The magazine *Shakmaty v. S.S.S.R.* conducted a wide-ranging discussion on the topic in 1952. A number of chess players contributed articles and letters in which good ideas were expressed, but up to now nobody has undertaken the serious task of writing a book on "The Theory of Combinations".

I am attracted by the idea of this work, but the present book is meant for ordinary players, and therefore there is no room here for deep theoretical research.

All the same I am convinced that from the very start of his study of the game, a player should not only assimilate various useful points from more experienced players, and study the accumulated experience of chess theory, but should also understand the heart of the matter, take account of the real content of this question and link it correctly with other problems of chess strategy and tactics.

Therefore, although there is no possibility of formulating a definitive theory of combinations in this book, we must try to lay down the essential foundations of such a theory. We shall examine a number of examples and will gradually make the necessary generalizations as we accumulate practical chess experience.

Diagram No. 1

In this position, White can play **1 f6**. After this there arises a **threat** of mate on **g 7** by the queen (We emphasize certain words to draw special attention to them).

Obviously, Black has only one defense, namely the **forced** move **1...g6**, but then White continues **2 Qh6** and renews his threat. It is easy to see that Black cannot avert mate. He can, in fact, defer it for one move by **2...Qxh3ch** but this of course makes no real difference.

Now another example (*Diagram No. 2*)

1   Ne7ch   Kh8

The only move if Black does not want to give up his

queen for a knight which would of course mean certain defeat.

2 Qxh7ch!

An unexpected stroke. White sacrifices his queen so
as to destroy the Black king's protection, which leads to
immediate mate. The destruction of the pawn cover of
the king is not significant in this particular case - only
one pawn is removed - but because of the characteristics of the position, because of the great activity of the
White pieces, this is enough to win.

2 ...   Kxh7

3 Rh3 mate

Let us compare the course of play of the two positions
we have examined.

In the first position, despite Black's great material advantage, White achieved victory in a way which caused
no surprise. Everything went "normally". After White's
first move his opponent was forced to weaken, in a decisive way, the pawn protection of his king. White immediately exploited this by penetrating with his queen
to **h6** which meant immediate mate. In the second example White, by sacrificing his queen, won in a special
way.

In actual fact in the "normal" course of play to give
up one's queen means the loss of the game, but here we
see that the giving away of the queen, which we call a
sacrifice in such cases, leads to an immediate win. Why
does this happen? The Black king is **exposed** to attack
and White gets a chance to mate with the pieces which
remain on the board. Hence by means of the queen sacrifice a special position was created in which the White
pieces achieved maximum activity.

In both cases we see the forced nature of all Black's
replies; he, in the given position, was the defending
side. But we repeat that in the first example White
achieves mate in a "normal" manner, and in the second
by a sacrifice.

We are going to call the first method a **forced maneuver**, that is a maneuver whereby the defending
side is forced to make moves which are imposed on him,
and the attacking side does not have recourse to any

sacrifice. We have already arrived at the principal definition in its general form: A forced maneuver or maneuvers combined with a sacrifice is what we call a combination. (*The knowledgeable reader will have noted that in making this definition Bondarevsky chooses to follow the example of Botvinnik who so defined a combination in 1939. His actual definition was "A combination is a forced variation with a sacrifice". This can be said to be the restricted definition, as there is a school of thought which prefers a wider definition. Thus one can quote another leading Soviet methodologist, Romanovsky, who in the second edition of his book on the middlegame published in 1963 wrote "The broad concept of a combination, which the chess classics held, can be expressed by the following simple definition: A combination is a forced variation by means of which its initiator achieves an aim which he sets out to reach"-B.C.*).

The Elements of Combination

In carrying out both a forced maneuver and a combination the active side, i.e. the one which starts the operation forces his opponent either to make the only possible move in reply (as in the above examples) or to choose one of a limited number of replies. In the latter case the forced maneuver consists not of one, but of several variations. It stands to reason that in a practical game only one of these variations occurs on the board and the remainder are merely calculated mentally. But in each of these variations the active side creates threats and forces definite replies until the variation finally ends to its advantage. This advantage can be mate (as above), the gain of material (of the queen, a rook, a pawn, etc) or even simply an improved position of one's pieces and pawns or deterioration of the opponent's.

Of course an advantage is ensured only when a *correct* forced maneuver or a correct combination is played. In practice it sometimes turns out that the active side does not get an objective advantage as a result of the combination, but merely creates a position which suits his tastes and his style of play. Such forced maneuvers or combinations are also correct, strictly speaking, but it is best to call them modifying maneuvers or combinations. All forced maneuvers or combinations, although conceived in the player's mind, are realized on the board not because they are thought up by this or that player, but because the actual position on the board allows them to be realized thanks to its special characteristics. These characteristics which regulate the possibility of playing a forced maneuver or combination we call **motifs**.

Motifs, as it were, suggest in what direction a player's thoughts should work. (It is very important to make use of this in one's practice). In certain cases these motifs can be inadequate for playing a forced maneuver or combination as they are insufficiently weighty. In other cases they are sufficiently weighty and so they serve as a good basis for indicating the direction of the main blow. The detailed study of forced maneuvers is equally important for practical play and for the study of combinations, but in this book such maneuvers will be studied only as elements of combinations.

Let us now examine in more detail what happened in example No. 2. In analyzing the position the passive position of the Black pieces, unable to take part in the defense of the king, strikes one forcibly. On the other hand the White pieces are superbly placed and can easily be employed in an attack on the king. Hence the direction of the main blow is clear. Apart from that the situation on the board is such that White has to act quickly and energetically before Black mobilizes his forces, as in that case the activity of the White pieces would be neutralized whereupon Black's material advantage would gradually, with correct play, decide the game in his favor. But it isn't enough that the situation should suggest the direction of the main blow and that energetic measures should be called for. One has to find a way to gain an advantage, exploiting for this purpose the available motifs, i.e. to find a concrete line which leads to an advantage. In every combination starting with a sacrifice the finding of the concrete line consists of two stages. First of all by means of a sacrifice a definite thought is realized, which we call the **idea** of the combination. This idea has as its aim the changing of the motifs in such a way as to get a position in which new motifs are exploited by a forced maneuver or by a certain move to gain an advantage. Let us explain this by an example.

(Diagram No. 3 White to move)

What drawbacks are there in the placing of the Black pieces, i.e. what motifs exist for a combination? One must say that generally speaking Black stands quite well. But combinations can exploit not only chronic weaknesses of a position but also little weaknesses which are not noticeable at first glance. Black has such a little weakness in his position here. His rook on d7 is unguarded. Well, what of it, is it really obligatory to have all one's pieces guarding each other? No, of course it isn't obligatory, but in this particular situation it turns out that this weakness can be exploited. One should note too the active disposition of White's pieces.

1 Rxf6

This sacrifice of the exchange realizes a definite thought - the idea of the combination. The Black g-pawn has to play onto the f-file, which opens the Black king to attack. Thus the idea of the combination lies in the diversion of the pawn from the g-file.

1 ...   g x f 6

After the realization of the idea a position with new motifs has been created. Now not just one object - the rook on d7 - but two objects - the king and rook - are subject to attack. This is achieved by White's next move which creates two attacks in two directions.

2 Qg4ch   Kh8
3 Qxd7

and White has won a piece.

In this particular example we saw a simple combination with one sacrifice, but in a complicated combination there can be several sacrifices with various ideas. Further on we shall also see cases where two ideas are realized by one sacrifice. The second stage of a combination, as already becomes clear from the example, realizes the motifs newly created by means of the sacrifice. The concluding move which exploits the new motifs we shall call the **resultant blow**. In this particular case 2 Qg4ch is such a blow. We shall call the position occurring after the resultant blow the **designated position**.

One must remark straight away that it is not always the case that the designated position coincides with the **final position**, which is assessed by us from the point of view of the final advantage. In the given example the final position occurs after 3 Qxd7 while the designated position occurs after 2 Qg4ch.

We have made a slight diversion and explained on the basis of a concrete example what the idea of a combination is, and what are the resultant blow, the designated position and the final position. Let us now return to the analysis of Diagram No. 2. What did the basic idea of the combination consist of? The idea consisted of opening up and partially destroying the Black king's position by a queen sacrifice. The king on h7 is exposed and is mated by the two remaining White pieces. Thus here the idea of destroying the king's position is carried out, admittedly to a fairly slight degree. In such simple positions with a minimal destruction of the king position one can also reckon that we have a case of the idea of drawing the king onto the very bad square h7. However, further on in cases of more complicated combinations which we consider in the second chapter, we shall see a fundamental difference between the ideas of destruction and diversion. In this case the forced maneuver is the single resultant blow - **Rh3 mate**, and the designated position occurring after it coincides with the final position.

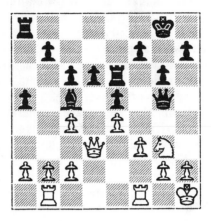

(Diagram No. 4 Delekta vs. Geller, Cappelle la Grande 1992. Black to move)

We observe here the powerful influence of the Black bishop on the a7-g1 diagonal. This diagonal keeps White's King "locked" in the corner. This gives rise to the idea of exploiting the king's position. If only we could give a check on the h-file it would be mate. This idea leads to the initial sacrifice.

1 ...   Qxg3!
2 hxg3

Otherwise White is just a piece down. But now the h-file is opened.

2 ...   g5

And suddenly White has no defense against 3...Rh6 mate.

(See Diagram No. 5)

Clearly Black has a menacing array of pieces pointing toward White's king. The two Black bishops exert withering pressure down their adjacent diagonals. The Ra8 and the Qg2 exert, respectively, vertical and lateral pressure focused against White's king. Finally the centralized Ne5 is more than willing to leap into the attack at the first opportunity; it is hardly surprising that Black has a winning sacrifice.

1 ...   Rxa4!

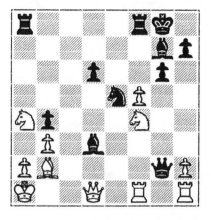

(Diagram No. 5 Zarovnjatov vs. Pankratov, correspondence game, 1990-2. Black to move)

The basic idea behind this sacrifice is to remove the knight's protection of the **Bb2**. This in turn will allow the following sacrifice which will lead to a mating attack.

2 bxa4

After **2 Nxd3 Nxd3** the Black knight unveils the action of the **Bg7** which, in conjunction with the **Qg2**, creates a threefold attack on **b2**. Note that in this case **3 Bxg7** allows the Black rook at **a4** and queen at **g2** to coordinate giving mate at **a2**. The capture of Black's queen by **2 Nxg2** is followed by **2...Rxa2ch! 3 Kxa2 Ra8ch 4 Ba3 Rxa3ch 5 Kb2 Nc4 dis. dbl. ch 6 Kc1 Ra1 mate** - note the completely forcing character of each of Black's moves in this sequence. The attempt to disrupt Black's combination by **2 Qxd3** fails after **2...Rxa2ch 3 Kxa2** (*Or 3 Kb1 Qxb2 mate*) **3...Qa8ch** (*Getting Black's queen out of range of the Nf4 with a compelling check*) and **4...Nxd3** wins.

2 ...   Qxb2ch!

Both removing a key "bodyguard" - the **Bb2** - and forcing the king into the open lines which will be under full control of the Black pieces.

3 Kxb2   Nc4 dis. dbl ch

Discovered double check is usually devastating.

4 Kb3

On 4 Kc1 the king's bishop swoops in for 4...Bb2 mate.

$$4 \quad ... \qquad Na5ch$$
$$5 \quad Kxb4$$

Forced. Note that a4 is not an available flight square for White's king - a subtle and essential point of Black's initial sacrifice 1...Rxa4.

$$5 \quad ... \qquad Rb8ch$$

And White has to resign in view of 6 Kxa5 Bc3 mate, or 6 Ka3 Bb2 (Or 6...Nc4) mate.

Thus in completing our analysis of the five combinations above we can already say that in every combination there are motives, ideas, sacrifices, forced maneuvers, the resultant blow, the designated position, final positions and the advantage.

The Sacrifice as a Basic Element of a Combination

Let us consider now in greater detail those sacrifices which form part of a combination. Generally speaking, when he makes a sacrifice the active player augments the power of his pieces with a special energy, and at the same time causes a lack of harmony in his opponent's pieces, destroys their cooperation, renders some of them unguarded and so on. One can say that after a sacrifice the activity, the power of one's pieces increases so much that it becomes possible, despite the opponent's material advantage, to achieve a final objective advantage by means of forcing moves, by moves which call forth definite replies.

When the final advantage is mate then, naturally enough, the amount of material sacrificed is unimportant. But what happens if the advantage is, say, the win of a piece? Can one in that case sacrifice one's queen? Obviously in this case too sacrifices are feasible. We shall see this later in concrete examples.

It is important to make clear that in a combination the pieces which remain after the sacrifice by means of forced maneuvers compel, with mathematical accuracy, no matter how long the combination may be, the defending side not only to return all the sacrificed material but also to finish up at a disadvantage - either materially or positionally.

From what has been said it is clear that in a combination the forced maneuver must occur after the sacrifice, but can also precede it, when there follows the sacrifice and then once again a forced maneuver. In other words the forced maneuvers before and after the sacrifice form, together with the sacrifice, a complete forced operation which we call a combination. It becomes feasible because of the appropriate motifs. In my opinion there is no reason in theory to divide the forced operation into its constituent parts as certain writers do, because for practical purposes it is important to establish and underline the indivisible link of all the parts of the operation, which are subordinated to a single aim and which arise on the basis of the motifs in the initial position. One can draw the analogy that at the time of the sacrifice in a combination chess "material" is transformed into "energy" which is subsequently transformed back into "material" by means of a forced maneuver with advantage for the active side. This analogy may seem rather far-fetched, but it reflects well the nature of the phenomena which occur in a combination. In short, simple, combinations everything happens very quickly. The forced maneuver is sometimes transformed into a single resultant blow, and only one piece gets a chance to display its "energy". In more complicated, longer combinations one can easily discern the great activity, "energy" of a number of pieces after the sacrifice.

The transformation of "material" into "energy" is followed by the reverse process only in correct combinations in which in the course of time measured in moves the energy imparted to the remaining pieces by the sacrifice is once again transformed into the usual material. One can say that a combination is a form of explosion on the chess board when the usual regular considerations lose their significance. For quiet, "normal" play we have a recognized measuring rod for assessing values. Long experience convinces us that a queen is about equal to two rooks or three minor pieces. A minor piece can be compensated for by three pawns and so on. If however a correct combination is played, then during the course of the combination, all these calculations have no significance. The decisive factor is the energy of the forces which are idea-directed towards the achievement of the final advantage. Only at the end of the combination do the usual relationships once again come into their own.

Let us now analyze another three positions.

(Diagram No. 6, Capablanca vs. Yates, New York 1924.
White to move)

> 1 Nc3   Rc5

Black must move his attacked rook onto this square as otherwise he would lose his 'a' pawn. Of course, he cannot play 1...Nxc3 because of 2 Rxd7ch and 3 Kxc3 when White is a piece up. This is a variation.

> 2 Ne4   Rb5

This and the following moves are also forced.

> 3 Ned6   Rc5
> 4 Nb7

Two attacks in two directions. White simultaneously attacks rook and 'a' pawn.

> 4 ...   Rc7
> 5 N7xa5

And White has won a pawn.

What have we seen in this example from the point of view of our theoretical considerations? Black had a weak 'a' pawn which was already attacked by the White knight in the initial position. The pawn was defended only by a rook whose choice of squares was strictly limited. These circumstances served as a motif which suggested to White where he should make his main threat and look for a forced continuation leading to the achievement of a clear advantage - the win of the 'a' pawn.

Can one call the forcing line which White chose a combination? No, because everything went "normally", without sacrifices, without breaking the normal considerations of chess "material". Hence in this case we merely have a forced maneuver.

(Diagram No. 7. White to move)

1 Nf7ch   Kg8

Forced; if **1...Rxf7**, **2 Qxc8ch** forces mate next move. This is a variation, though admittedly a very simple one.

2 Nh6 dis. dbl. ch   Kh8

Now White has a draw by repeating his forced maneuver. However the Black king's position is very restricted and he is being attacked by two White pieces. This is a motif for seeking an idea that can bring an advantage. Such an idea can be found here!

3 Qg8ch!

A queen sacrifice to restrict the king to the maximum degree, to block him with his own pieces. For this purpose the rook is drawn onto g8. At the same time the rook is **diverted** from its guard of f7. Hence the combinational idea consists of **blocking** by attraction in one case and **diversion** in the other, both achieved by a single sacrifice.

3 ... **R x g 8**
4 Nf7 mate

The advantage - mate - has been achieved. A single knight move has finished the game exploiting to the maximum degree the restriction of the Black king which was already under attack. Such a mate is called "smothered mate". There is no need here to ask what has taken place - a forced maneuver or a combination.

Four of the positions we have examined are quoted in Emanuel Lasker's *Chess Manual.* We have repeated them, with quite different comments, in order to stress the differing attitude of writers to the concept of a combination. Lasker saw no difference in principle between these examples and regards them as combinations.

(Diagram No. 8. Wahls vs. Yusupov, Germany 1992.
Black to move)

The most important feature of this position is Black's forward 'g' pawn. The presence of a 'g' pawn at **g 3** (*Or* *g6 - if White is the attacker)* quite often gives rise to winning combinative play. However, in order to take advantage of this, Black must open lines - in particular the h-file - to allow Black's queen and rooks to invade with decisive threats. This reasoning gives us the correct first move:

1 ...   h 3 !

It must be noted that there are no <u>immediate</u> threats, but clearly Black will invade down the h-file with ...Rh5 and ...hxg2 soon if White stands by idly.

2 hxg3

White adopts a "show me" attitude, intending to play Kg2 and Rh1 to barricade the position.

2 ...   Qh7!

The star move, offering a sacrifice of the important 'g' pawn. Note Black's first two moves have been pawn sacrifices; remember the basic theme here is to open lines for Black's heavy pieces.

3 Kg2

Here we reach an important juncture, White having two choices. The idea behind the text move is obvious: defend the 'h' pawn and thus block Black's h-file intentions. But what if White accepts the offer of the g 3 pawn? The answer is **3 Rxg3 Qxh3!** (*Note the pins which disallow both 4 Rxh3 - because it's illegal - and 4 Rxg7 Qxe3ch) 4 Rf3 (Or 4 Kf2 Qh2ch forcing the win of the Rg3)* 4...Rh5 5 Rxg7 *(On 5 Kf2 Qh1 6 Qc5 Rh2ch 7 Ke3 Qe1ch 8 Kd4 Qe4 mates - the invasion down the h-file quickly transforms itself into a mating attack)* 5...Qh1ch 6 Kf2 Rh2ch 7 Kg3 and now both 7...Qg2 and 7...Rg2 are mate.

3 ...   R h 5

With the simple idea of 4...Rxh3 consistently breaking through down the h-file. However, this move is actually a double threat since now the h 7 - b 1 diagonal is cleared for the queen. Now, if 4 Rh1 to defend h3 then 4...Qc2ch wins since 5 Kf1! allows the thrust 5... g 2 c h .

4 Rxg3

The 'g' pawn must be taken,

4 ...   R x h 3 !

Again we see a double pin - as after Black's ...Qxh3 i n

the note to White's **3 Kg2.**

5 Rxg7

Defense by **5 Rf3** is refuted by **5...Rh2ch 6 Kf1** (*6 Kg1 Rh1ch 7 Kf2 Qh2ch 5 Rg2 Qxg2 - or Rxg2 mate*) **6...Qb1ch 7 Qe1 Rh1ch** wins.

          5 ...   **R h 2 c h**

          6 Kg1

The try **6 Kf3** loses to **6...Qh5ch 7 Rg4** (*7 Kg3 Qh3 is mate*) **7...Rh3ch** wins White's queen.

          6 ...   **R h 1 c h**

          7 Kf2

On **7 Kg2 Qh2ch 8 Kf3 Rxf1ch.**

          7 ...   **Q c 2 c h**

Again the **h7-b1** diagonal comes into play.

          8 Kg3

If **8 Qe2** then **8...Rh2ch 9 Rg2 Rxg2ch.**

          8 ...   **Q h 2 c h**

Now if **9 Kf3** then   **9...Rxf1ch.**

          9 Kg4   **Q h 5 c h**

        10 Kg3   **Q h 3 c h**

And White gave up since **11 Kf2 Qxf1ch 12 Kg3 Rh3ch 13 Kg4 Qg2ch 14 Qg3 Qxg3** is mate.

Before passing on to further explanation of the important features of combinations, I would like to deal with a point which has no direct relationship to the theory of combinations, but which is interesting from a general point of view. Doubtless the reader who has carefully examined the examples quoted will have reacted to them differently. I imagine that the forced maneuvers seemed to him very logical and consequential, but for all that, I rather think that they will not have moved him much, not called forth any esthetic response. The combinations, however, for all their simplicity, will have caused his heart to beat faster, I am sure, if this is the first time that he has seen them. We shan't be dealing with esthetic questions in this book, but I regard it as necessary to mention this difference in response.

What I have noted is a very characteristic factor which stresses the difference between a forced maneuver and a combination, not from a theoretical point of view, but with regard to the artistic effect on a player, from the viewpoint of chess beauty. The main role in this is played by the basic element of combination - the sacrifice. As we have already established, every combination consists of a number of elements. In this book we shall devote considerable attention to the basic element of sacrifice, and Chapter II will deal with it. Now we have to familiarize ourselves with two other points which are closely linked with every combination.

The Calculation of a Combination and the Assessment of the Final Position

One begins a combination only when one has clearly calculated mentally all the forced moves, reckoned with all possible replies, i.e. when one has considered all variations to the very end, to the final position, to the point where the normal relationships and assessments again come into play. Just as they did before the "explosion" of the combination.

It stands to reason that an error in one's calculations is irreparable, and in this case the combination becomes incorrect. In other words despite the presence of a definite idea no advantage is obtained, rather on the contrary the active side comes off worse. Why does this happen? Because the motifs which seemed adequate for playing the combination in actual fact were not adequate and the mental calculation turns out to be an optical illusion because of the mistake. As a result the sacrifice was pointless and the process of transforming matter into energy is not subsequently reversed. The inadequate energy of the pieces gained as a result of the sacrifice is gradually dissipated when it meets accurate defense from the defending side and then his material advantage decides the game.

Where the mental calculation of the combination is correct, one must first, before playing the intended move, carefully, assess the final position in every variation, to establish whether they are really advantageous. If not then of course the combination is pointless. Let us first explain the essential features of the mental calculation and then return to the assessment of the final position. Here are some examples of the necessity of accurate calculation.

(Diagram No. 9. Capablanca vs. Tanarov, New York 1918. White to move)

In assessing the position we note the fine placing of all the White pieces. Whereas Black is cramped and moreover has a weak 'd' pawn which he has to defend with his pieces. White stands better. The weakness of the 'd' pawn, already attacked by rook and knight, and the disposition of his queen and bishop along the diagonal of the Black knight and 'd' pawn seemed to Capablanca to be sufficient motives for a combination, whose idea as we shall see, is to **attract** the Black rook to **d6** where it is pinned. Capablanca envisaged exploiting this pin by his resultant blow. Let us first see what happened in the game.

1 Rxd6

With this sacrifice Capablanca starts his combination. Note that 1 Nxd6 Rxd6 2 Bxe5 could be refuted by 2...Rxd1 threatening   mate.

1 ...   Rxd6

2 Bxe5

Now the pinned rook seems doomed as after 2...Bxe5 3 Qxe5 White wins because of a double attack - on the rook and the mate threat on g7.

2 ...   Rd1?

3 Rxd1   Bxe5

The combination is completed, White has won the 'd' pawn, but Capablanca immediately begins a second combination which at once decides the game. On 3...Qxe5 White would have continued just as in the game.

4 Nh6ch   Kh8
5 Qxe5!

The motive for this combination is the situation of the Black king, hemmed in by his own pawns. By sacrificing his queen White **attracts** the Black queen to **e5 and** at the same time **diverts** it from **d8** from the defense of the back row.

5 ...   Qxe5
6 Nxf7ch

The sacrifice **diverts** the rook from the back row and simultaneously delivers the resultant blow, or rather a double blow, check and an attack on the queen. The knight cannot be taken because of 7 Rd8 and mate. The motive of the combination - the hemmed in position of the king - is seen very clearly in this variation. If however the king moves out of check then simply 7 Nxe5 and White is a piece up. Hence Tanarov resigned.

Capablanca's two combinations in succession make a strong impression, but analysis shows the first one was incorrect! If Tanarov had played 2...Qa5 instead of 2...Rd1 then Capablanca would not have gotten any advantage from his combination, on the contrary his position would have been worse than when he started.

A few variations: 3 f4 Bxe5 4 fxe5 Qc5ch 5 Kh1 Rg6 and Black is the exchange up. Or 3 Bc3 Bxc3 4 Qxd6 Bxe1 5 Ne7ch Kh8 6 Nxc6 Bxf2ch 7 Kxf2 Qb6ch and so, also to Black's advantage. Another White try is 3 Nh6ch Kh8 4 Bc3 but then 4...Bxc3 5 Qxd6 Bb4 follows.

White, having convinced himself that all these variations are bad for him, would have to play 3 Bc3 Bxc3 4 bxc3 Rg6 5 Ne7ch Kh8 6 Nxg6ch hxg6. In the resulting position White would have lost the advantage which he enjoyed before his combination. Black would have very good drawing chances, because of the chronic weakness of White's queenside pawns. In this particular case Capablanca was lucky, as his incorrect calculation of the combination did not turn out too badly for him, but as a rule such an error results in very unpleasant consequences.

We have quoted this example to convince the reader of the need for painstaking calculation, for the keenest attention, when he is contemplating a combination. As you see, even such a player as Capablanca was not sufficiently alert and went in for a doubtful combination.

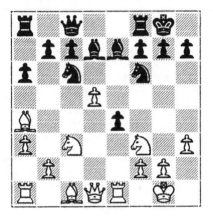

(Diagram No. 10. Gufeld vs. Klovan, Moscow 1956. Black to move)

       1 ...   Rd8?

Black by sacrificing his knight starts a combination based on the idea of freeing the file on which the White queen stands opposite the Black rook. However he has calculated the combination badly.

       2 dxc6!   Bxh3

The quite harmless 'point' of the combination.

       3 cxb7!   Qg4

       4 Nh4!

If now **4...Rxd1** then White wins either by **5 bxa8 =Qch** or by **5 Bxd1.**

       4 ...   Qxh4

       5 bxa8=Q Rxa8

       6 g3

The simplest, as White forces the exchange of queens and remains a rook up. In both cases incorrect calculation created the illusion that the available motifs were sufficient for making a combination. But it sometimes happens that the motifs are adequate, there is a good idea available but the combinative opportunity is missed because of a failure in calculation.

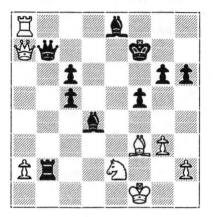

(Diagram No. 11. Ragozin vs. Alatortsev, 10th USSR Ch. 1937. White to move)

Under the influence of his opponent's material advantage, White refrains from making the necessary calculations at a time when he had a chance of going in for a winning combination.

1 Nxd4   cxd4

Nothing is altered by **1...Rb1ch 2 Kf2** as he cannot continue **2...Rb2ch** because of **3 Ne2.**

2 Qxb7ch   Rxb7

3 Rxe8

The idea of the combination is to attract the king onto a bad square with respect to the position of the Black rook.

3 ...   Kxe8

If **3...Rb1ch** then **4 Re1** and White's material advantage is enough to win the game.

4 Bxc6ch

The resultant blow - once again a double attack as in the Capablanca-Tanarov game.

4 ...   Rd7

5 Ke2

White should win the resulting pawn ending. For example **5...g5 6 Kd3 f4 7 gxf4.** Let us take the opportunity and draw the reader's attention to the order of moves in the combination. White first exchanged minor pieces and then queens. If he had started with the queen exchange, then Black would have had a defense, **1 Qxb7ch Rxb7 2 Nxd4** (*Or 2 Rxe8*) **2...Rb1ch** and so on. Thus in carrying out a combination, one must ensure that the order of moves envisaged in the mental calculation is kept to. Now let us consider the factors which accompany every calculation.

What are the means of **compulsion** in a combination? We have been talking about the fact that the active side all the time compels definite replies. How is this done? It is valuable to explain here what means are employed in this compulsion process and which of them are forcing to the greatest degree. First and foremost every checking move is the highest degree of compulsion. Then the number of possible replies can be sharply restricted by a threat of mate, though it is not as forcing as a check. In fact when one is threatened with mate one can still undertake any advantageous operation as long as it is accompanied by checks. Hence when playing a combination one must not reckon that a threat of mate will automatically force the opponent to defend against it. This can well be a miscalculation as the defending side may then unexpectedly go over to active operations and by a counter-combination or forced maneuver, ignore the threat and force an advantage. Let us convince ourselves of this on the basis of the following example.

(See Diagram No. 12)

Black is not merely threatening mate, but seems to have created a threat against which there is no defense. In actual fact he erred in going into this position as White has a chance to mate first by a combination consisting entirely of checks.

1 Rh8ch

At first sight this only defers mate, but in fact the rook sacrifices **attract** the Black king to **h8** and at the same time **vacate** the square **h1** so that the White queen can decisively come into play.

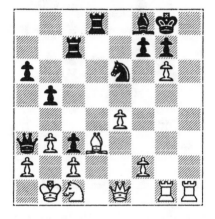

(Diagram No. 12. White to move)

1	...	K x h 8
2	Rh1ch	Kg8
3	Rh8ch	K x h 8
4	Qh1ch	

and mate next move on h7.

The defender's replies are considerably reduced by an attack on various pieces or pawns or by the threat of such an attack. Moreover it is understandable that an attack on the queen forces its defense or the creation of a counter-threat greater in strength or equal to an attack on the queen, such as a check or a threat of mate. Of course a threat of equal strength would be a counter-attack on the opponent's queen. Let us now show how the threat of an attack without the actual threat itself can compel the opponent to defend, considerably restricting his choice of moves.

(See Diagram No. 13)

By playing 1 Nf1 White threatens the fork 2 Ne3. Black must defend against this either by moving his queen or his rook on **d5** otherwise he would lose the exchange.

But we have not exhausted the various means of compulsion. The capture of any piece or pawn for the purpose of exchanging also compels the opponent either to

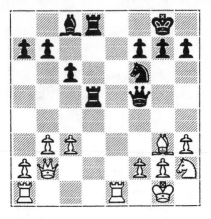

(Diagram No. 13. White to move)
make the one move that enables him to re-establish material equality or to choose for the same purpose one of a restricted number of moves. For example in the following position which occurs in a variation of the Ruy Lopez after a mistake by Black.

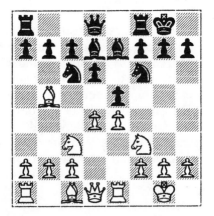

(Diagram No. 14. White to move)
White now wins by a forced maneuver which uses exchanges as a means of compulsion.

1 Bxc6   Bxc6

Forced, as if 1...bxc6 2 dxe5 wins a pawn. Black's next move is likewise forced.

2 dxe5	d x e 5
3 Qxd8	

If White captures the 'e' pawn straight away Black replies **3...Qxd1** followed by **4...Bxe4** winning back the pawn.

3 ...	R a x d 8

Black also gets a lost position after 3...**Rfxd8 4 Nxe5 Bxe4** (*Not 4...Nxe4 because of 5 Nxc6*) **5 Nxe4 Nxe4** (*Black has now won back the pawn as the knight cannot be captured because of back row mate. However Black has merely got out of the frying pan into the fire*) **6 Nd3** (*Now the two undefended Black pieces on the open file are placed very awkwardly*) **6...f5 7 f3 Bc5 c h** (*All forced*) **8 Kf1.** Now Black can try **8...Rf8** hoping for **9 fxe4 fxe4ch 10 Nf4 g5**,etc. But the simple **9 Ke2** then forces considerable material advantage, e.g. **9...Bb6 10 fxe4 fxe4 11 Nf4 g5 12 Nh3** and so on.

4 Nxe5	B x e 4
5 Nxe4	N x e 4
6 Nd3	f 5
7 f3	B c 5 c h

All of these Black moves are forced if he wants to maintain material equality. **8 Nxc5 Nxc5 9 Bg5.** Now White wins the exchange. For example **9...Rd5 10 Be7** (*This is also played against other rook moves*) **10...Re8 11 c4** and Black's best now is to give up the exchange.

Finally there is one more means of compulsion which is linked with the very essence of combination, namely the sacrifice. The fact that a sacrifice forces definite replies is clear without examples, as we have already seen cases of this.

Hence there is a huge arsenal of the means of compulsions. The important point is merely to choose the most effective means in each concrete position without over-estimating the available degree of compulsion.

(See Diagram No. 15)

Black here supposed that White could not make a combination with the idea of **destroying   the   defense** of the **Rd3** by **1 Rxc5** and convinced himself of this by the following line of reasoning: "If rook takes my knight I obviously don't recapture with the bishop as then my rook is unguarded and *en prise* to his rook. Instead I take his rook on d2 and in order not to lose material he will have to play Nxd2 when I shall play ...Bxc5 and so finish up with the exchange to the good". All of this line of reasoning is incorrect as Black did not consider all White's possible replies after **1 Rxc5 Rxd2** from the point of view of compulsion.

(Diagram No. 15. White to move)

Considering the position carefully we see that White can play a move of the highest degree of compulsion - **2 Rh5ch**, getting his rook away from the attack of the bishop. Black must defend against the check and instead of Black winning the exchange White wins a piece.

Moves like **2 Rh5ch** are called intermediate checks, and one must always take account of them in calculating combinations. Of course it is not just an intermediate move that can cause a breakdown in our calculation - any reply which has a greater degree of compulsion is by its nature an intermediate move. Obviously we must pay attention to all such moves. In connection with the fact that the moves of a combination have different degrees of compulsion we have the case of the "desperado" piece.

Here is an example:

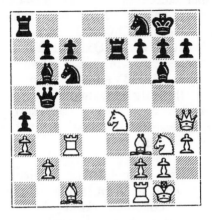

(Diagram No. 16. White to move)

1 Rxc6

White plays a combination based on *destroying the defense* of the Re7, as if 1...bxc6 then 2 Qxe7. However after the capture of the knight Black is not compelled to take the rook and can look for a move of an equal or greater degree of compulsion which may allow him to guard his rook indirectly.

Examine for example the reply 1...Bxe4 whereby Black replies to White's capture of a knight by the capture of an equivalent piece. Then after 2 Qxe7 Bxc6 Black has lost nothing. Hence now we must examine alternative second moves by White. First of all there is the recapture on e4 by knight or bishop. Try 2 Bxe4. Now once again 2...bxc6 is bad because of 3 Qxe7 and White has realized his aim. But Black instead can play 2...Rxe4 getting his rook away from capture with a greater degree of compulsion as he attacks the queen. Only on the capture of this rook would Black reply 3...bxc6. White could try 3 Rxb6 instead, so creating an equivalent threat, as the Black queen is now *en prise* as well. Both 3...Rxh4 4 Rxb5 and 3...Qxb6 4 Qxe4 leave White a piece up. However in playing 3 Rxb6 White has not reckoned with a Black move which has a greater degree of compulsion, namely 3...Qxf1ch!. It is in connection with such unexpected strokes that one speaks of the "desperado". In this case the Black queen for just one move is a desperado. After **4 Kxf1 Rxh4** Black is the exchange up. Now consider **2 Nxe4** instead of **2 Bxe4**. Then here too there follows **2...Rxe4**. Once again **3 Rxb6** is bad because of **3...Qxf1ch!** By means of **3 Qxe4 bxc6 4 Qxc6** White can win just a pawn. So we have established that after **1...Bxe4** the recapture on e 4 does not give White the big advantage he was playing for when he started his combination. But surely the rook on c 6 can also be a desperado? What about **2 Rxb6!** - White wins two pieces for a rook.

We see from these examples that a piece can become a desperado at the very moment when it seems doomed to capture. We must conclude from the variations above that there is no point in Black replying to **1 Rxc6** by **1...Bxe4**. Notice now that after **1 Rxc6** the Black rook is in a doomed situation. Why shouldn't he then become a desperado? So...

1 ...   Rxe4!

Once again White cannot 'desperado" his "doomed" rook on **c6** by **2 Rxb6** because of **2...Qxf1ch!** when once again Black wins the exchange. Instead White would have to reply to **1...Rxe4** by **2 Nxe4** when **2... bxc6** leaves Black on equal terms.

We have already said that an attack on a piece or pawn is a means of compulsion. It is very useful to dwell in greater detail on the various sorts of attacks which are produced by different moves. One must note that the most valuable moves from the point of view of compulsion (as a rule, of course, but not always) are moves which are linked with attacks on two objects instead of one. In such cases the means of defense are more limited. In some positions there are no means of defense at all.

(See Diagram No. 17)
1 c4

This simultaneously attacks rook and queen. Obviously this forces the only possible reply **1...Qxc4**. Hence by means of a double attack even a pawn can serve to create the greatest possible degree of compulsion. White replies to **1...Qxc4** by **2 Ne3** and Black has no defense

(Diagram No. 17. White to move)

against this new double attack. As a result of the combination Black loses the exchange for a pawn. Hence in this particular case we have had a small combination with the idea of attracting the queen onto c4 by means of a double attack and the resultant blow is, again, a double attack.

(Diagram No. 18. White to move)

What can play 1 Bf4. With a single move he creates a double attack in two directions by means of two pieces, rook and bishop. In the previous example after 1 c4 there was also a double attack but by means of a single pawn. Apart from that one can create a double threat in one direction only by two pieces. As an example, one can cite any double check.

All the three methods which have been enumerated carry the general name in chess literature of double attack, which strictly speaking is incorrect. Hence whenever one comes across this expression one must note carefully the exact characteristics of the double attack, to understand more exactly what is taking place on the board. Returning to Diagram No. 18, note that after 1 Bf4 only one reply, 1...Rd7 maintains material equality. But if White's 'c' pawn were on c4 then White by means of 1 Bb4, a double attack in two directions, would win the exchange straight away.

We have already noted that it is by no means essential that some sort of double attack should be required for success. Sometimes a simple attack can be more effective, but as a rule it is more difficult to defend against the various sorts of double attacks.

What has been said about double attacks as a means of compulsion is also entirely the case with a resultant blow. Practice shows that it is a frequent occurrence that the resultant blow is a double attack. We shall have occasion to draw attention to this in considering further positions.

We have spent a long time considering the factors connected with the calculation of a combination, in view of their great importance. Let us move on to another important question - the assessment of the final position. It must be quite clear that the fate of the whole combination depends on a correct assessment of each of the final positions resulting from different variations of the combination. If only one of these positions is assessed incorrectly then the opponent can discover this and choose just this one variation in which the active side has erred.

Let us now examine to begin with, the type of position in which assessment of the position can give rise to controversy.

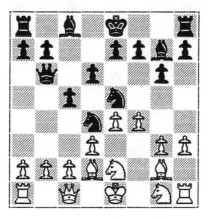

(Diagram No. 19. Smyslov vs Bronstein, XIX USSR Ch
1951. Black to move)

1 ... Nxc2ch

Black starts a combination instead of simply bringing
his attacked knight back to c6. The idea of the sacrifice
lies in *destroying the guard* of the White 'd' pawn.

2 Qxc2 Qxb2

A queen sacrifice with the idea of attracting the White
queen onto b2.

3 Qxb2 Nxd3ch

The resultant blow, attacking in two directions.

4 Kf1!

Better than 4 Kd1 Nxb2ch 5 Kc2 Nc4!

4 ... Bxb2

If 4...Nxb2 White can reply 5 Bc3 exchanging bishops to his advantage.

5 Rb1

Black's combination is concluded, and now one must
assess the final position. Although Black has three
pawns for his knight the position is still fairly complicated, and therefore White holds the advantage. The further course of the game fully confirmed this. Hence one
must regard Black's combination as unsound.

White went in for the following combination, reckoning to win a pawn.

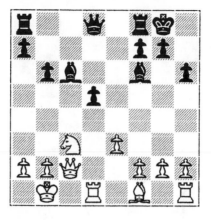

(Diagram 20. Sokolsky vs. Vasilyev, semi-final XVI USSR
Ch 1947. White to move)

1 Nxd5?

The knight **attracts** the bishop onto **d 5** where White
calculates he can win it by a simple attack to which
Black has no defense because of the pin on the bishop
which has now arisen.

1 ...   Bxd5
2 Bc4

The resultant blow. Now if **2...Rc8 3 Rxd5** and White
remains a pawn up. In this variation Sokolsky correctly
assessed the final position, but...

2 ...   Bxc4!
3 Rxd8   Raxd8
4 Qxc4

In this variation however, which Black in fact chose,
the final position was incorrectly assessed by White.
Despite his material advantage White is badly off, as the
Black pieces are very active, as we see from the further
course of the game.

4 ...   Rd2
5 b4

It is understandable that White's presence of mind
deserts him, and he loses quickly. A better move was **5
Re1**.

5 ...   R8d8
6 Re1   b5

7 Qxb5   Rc8
8 Resigns

The Genesis and Logical Nature of Combinations

Having become acquainted with the basic elements which make up a combination we must also elucidate an important point to do with combinations in general. How does a combination arise? Does it turn up by chance, or is it prepared for by the play preceding it? For the chess practitioner it is very important to work out the correct answer to these questions. The great chess theoretician, ex-world champion Dr. M. Euwe, in his book *Strategy and Tactics in Chess* made an attempt to divide all combinations into accidental and systematic combinations.

I cannot agree with such a division, as I consider all combinations to be logical. As we have already remarked, a combination does not arise because of the **talent** of this or that player. The given position on the board, its special features, its motifs as we have agreed to call them, govern the possibility of a combination's existence. The player "merely" has to know how to **find** the combination, employing the sharpness of his combinational vision. Hence if there are sufficient motifs, then a combination objectively exists. It is justified. On the one hand master games often develop so that as outcome of the struggle one side achieves a positional advantage as a result of which weaknesses arise in his opponent's position, the defender's pieces in defending these weaknesses become poorly placed, uncoordinated, etc. It is in just these cases that there arise motifs essential to the carrying out of a combination. One can say that one side has created motifs for carrying out a combination by consistent positional play. On the other hand it sometimes turns out that a weakness is created in one's position or the co-operation of one's pieces is destroyed as a result of a single weak move; or motifs for carrying out a combination may be created in some other way. Then one can speak of motifs which have arisen suddenly. Let us explain these considerations by examples.

(Diagram 21. Botvinnik vs. Euwe, World Ch. Match
Tournament 1948. White to move)

In this game Euwe had been in difficulties right from
the opening, and Botvinnik had exploited very well the
advantages of his situation and by consistent play had
achieved the diagramed position. In assessing this position we notice that the Black king is in danger because
of his exposed position, and that the Black rook is out of
play. Hence, there exist motifs for a combination. The
motifs suggest the direction of the main attack - one has
to create threats against the king and rook. These motifs
are the result of planned, consistent play by White.

1 Qg3!

The queen aims for **g7**; the idea of the knight sacrifice
is the *occupation* of a vital square.

1	...	f x e 5
2	Qg7	R f 8
3	Rc7	

If Black now defends against mate by 3...Qd6 then 4
Rxb7, e.g. 4...d3 5 Ra7 Qd8 6 Qxh7 with the decisive
threat of **7 Qg6ch.**

3	...	Qxc7
4	Qxc7	

White's combination beginning with **1 Qg3** is now
concluded. He enjoys a material advantage sufficient to
win by technique.

(Diagram No. 22. Kavalek vs. Martinovic, Sarajevo, 1968.
White to move)

Here again we shall emphasize the logical basis for White's combination. Both White rooks bear down against Black's king, which is thinly defended by only one pawn. Also note both White bishops are directed toward Black's king. With an initial sacrifice White is able to break through Black's limited defenses.

1 Rxg6!

Blowing away Black's only pawn defender and preparing to take advantage of the position of Black's queen.

1 ...   Nxg6

Essentially forced. If 1...Qf7 then 2 Qh2 is overwhelming, e.g. 2...Qe7 3 Qh7ch Kf7 4 Rxg7ch winning, or 2...Rfd8 3 Qh8 is mate. Also if 1...Qe7 then again 2 Qh2 is too strong - 2...Nxg6 3 Qh7ch Kf7 4 Qxg6ch Kg8 5 Rh8ch! Kxh8 6 Qh7 mate.

2 Bg5

Now in the actual game, Black tried 2...Qxf3 but after 3 Bxf3 Rxf3 4 Qh2 White has a winning position. For example 4...Raf8 5 Qh7ch Kf7 6 Rh6! (*A clever utilization of the h-file*) and now if 6...Nf4 then 7 Rf6ch! Ke8 8 Qxg7 wins. Or if 6...Nh8 then 7 Re6! and 8 Re7ch with attack on g7 is decisive since 7...Rg8 8 Qh5ch wins. After 2 Bg5 Black could have tried 2...Qf7 but then 3 Qh2 wins. For example, 3...Bh8 4 Bxg6 Qxg6 5 Qxh8ch Kf7 6 Rh7ch Ke8 7 Re7ch Kd8 8

Qxf8ch and mate next.

(Diagram No. 23. Botvinnik vs. Pachman, Moscow 1947.
White to move)

White played:

1   Rg5?

There followed:

1 ...   Rxe3!

If now 2 fxe3 simply 2...Qxg5 -*the exchange sacrifice has destroyed the defender* - while if 2 Qxe3 then the queen has been attracted onto a bad square and 2...Bf4 decides matters. As a result of the combination Black is left a piece up. What can we say about this particular case? By his incorrect first move White suddenly created the motifs for a combination. We repeat: motifs can occur in different ways; as a result of consistent play or suddenly but the combination is always justified.

From this last example we can also draw some conclusions essential in practical play. One must always, in *all* positions, analyze diligently. One must scrupulously weigh all the available motifs, as otherwise one might well overlook the chance of a combination. Even if you have been stubbornly defending for a long time and are still in a difficult position, the possibility of making a profitable combination has by no means disappeared. Even when your opponent has a great advantage he can still make a tactical mistake and by a careless move suddenly create motifs for you to make a perfectly logical combination. Here is a good example of this:

(Diagram No. 24. Levenfish vs. Checkover, Moscow 1935.
White to move)

White has a decisive advantage. He could adopt the forced maneuver **1 Rxg7ch Rxg7 2 Qxg7ch Qxg7 3 Bxg7 Kxg7** with a pawn ending in which his extra pawn guarantees the win. For example **4 Kg3 e5 5 Kf3 Kf6 6 Ke4 Ke6 7 h5 Kxd6 8 Kf5** and White must win. We recommend the reader to analyze this position carefully and convince himself that this is so. In passing we would remark that the analysis of pawn endings, in which one must calculate variations very exactly is useful in mastering the technique of analysis which certainly helps in developing one's combinational powers.

Grandmaster Levenfish, of course, saw this forced maneuver, but, it seems, decided that he had no need to hurry matters and had time to strengthen his position.

1 b4

White intends to play the indicated forced maneuver next move. The difference would be that in that case in the pawn ending which we gave in the last note, White could defend his 'd' pawn at the appropriate moment by c5. However, there is a tactical weakness in the placing of the White pieces, consisting of the fact that the queen is carrying out two important tasks - defending both the 'f' pawn and 'h' pawn which form a protective shield for the White king. Thus by his careless **1 b4** he makes a tactical mistake which suddenly presents his opponent with a chance to exploit the overloading of the queen.

1 ...   e5!

The idea behind this pawn sacrifice is clearly to divert the White queen from the the defense of either the 'f' pawn or the 'h' pawn. Black's combination of course is therefore quite logical.

2 Rxg7ch

This is what White chose in the game and after **2...Qxg7 3 Qd5 Qf6** soon led to loss for White. Other second moves for White were also unsatisfactory, for example **2 Qxe5 Qxh4ch 3 Kg2 Rxf2 mate** or **2 Qg4 Rxf2ch 3 Rg2** (*3 Kh1, then simply 3...Rxb2*) **3... Rxg2ch 4 Qxg2** (*4 Kxg2 Qd2ch and 5...Qxb2*) **4... Qxh4ch** with great advantage in the ending.

(*Bondarevsky's advice to be always on one's guard fits particularly well here as in the chess newspaper "Shakhmatnaya Moskva" in late 1965, a vigilant Russian amateur Korogodov suggested a stronger second move for White, namely 2 Qe4, as then 2...Rxf2ch 3 Kh1 Rxb2 loses to 4 Qa8ch Kf7 5 Rf1ch Kg6 (5...Ke6 6 Qd5 mate) 6 Qe4ch Kh5 7 Rg1! with decisive threats. Nor does 3...Rf4 work, crushing though it looks: 4 Rxg7ch! Qxg7 5 Qxf4 exf4 6 Bxg7 Kxg7 with the better game for White, or in this 4...Kxg7 5 Bxe5ch Rf6 6 Bb2! Kg8 7 Bxf6 and 8 Qe8ch again is better for White. Black's correct line is 3...Qe6 when Korogodov gives 4 Rg3, claiming that White stands better because of the variation 4...Rxb2 5 Qa8ch Kf7 6 Rf3ch Kg6 7 Qe4ch Kh5 8 Rg3!. However as the newspaper comments, in this line Black can improve by 6...Nf5 7 Qe4 Kf6 when if 8 Qg4, then not 8...h6 9 Qh5! but 8...e4! 9 Qg5ch Ke5 10 Qf4ch Kd4 11 Qxf5 Rb1ch 12 Kh2 Qxf5 13 Rxf5 e3 and Black wins. Obviously such a long variation cannot be regarded as exhaustive, and our conclusion must be that this example is obviously much more complicated than Bondarevsky thought- B.C.*).

Traps

Apart from forced maneuvers and combinations, the

arsenal of chess tactics also contains the resource known as "traps".

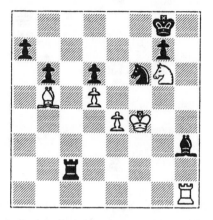

(Diagram No. 25. Bondarevsky vs. Ufimtsev, Leningrad 1936. Black to move.)

In this position Black made the quite "natural" move:

1 ...   **B g 2**

attacking the rook and the e 4 pawn. He had no suspicion that he was thus falling into a cunning trap. There followed:

    2   **Rh8ch**   **K f 7**
    3   **Be8ch!**   **N x e 8**
    4   **Kg5**

And Black has no defense against **5 Rf8** mate. The combination beginning **2 Rh8ch** had the idea of diverting the Black knight from f 6 by the bishop sacrifice, as once Black cannot play ...Nxe4ch the White king can safely play on to g5.

(See Diagram No. 26)

White could decide matters in his favor by **1 Qh2**. If then 1...e3 dis ch then 2 Kg3; Black has no check and only by the surrender of much material can he avert the threat of mate. White could also win by **1 Qe3**, for example 1...Rd3 2 Qb6 e3 dis.ch 3 Kh2 when once again there are no checks and there is no defense against **4 Rxh6ch**. With both players in severe time trouble White actually played:

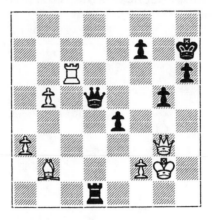

(Diagram No. 26. Smyslov vs. Tal, Candidates'
Tournament 1959. White to move.)

1 Qe5?

A move like this is quite "natural" when one has no
time to think. White threatens mate, and threatens to exchange queens which would force Black to resign. But it
was just such a "natural" move as this that Tal was reckoning on for a chance to set a clever trap.

1 ...   Rg1ch!

Black sacrifices his rook to **attract** the king onto the
back rank, when he can give check on **d1** and follow up
with perpetual check, e.g. **2 Kxg1 Qd1ch 3 Kh2
Qh5ch 4 Kg3 Qf3ch**, etc, but not **4...Qh4ch 5 Kg2
Qg4ch 6 Qg3.**

2 Kh2   Rh1ch

3 Draw

It follows from these examples that a trap involving a
sacrifice differs from a combination in that the first
move of the active player, i.e. the player who thinks up
the trap does not *force* the opponent's reply, but only
tempts him by some bait and so hopes to lure him onto
the wrong path. But once the "bait" has worked, then
there follows a genuine combination.

We have now finished considering the basic theory of
chess combinations and pass on to studying the various
ideas which underlie them.

Chapter II

Combinational Ideas

The number of possible chess combinations is astronomical. From the mathematical point of view the number is finite, just as the number of possible games is finite, but from a practical point of view one can confidently state that the number is infinitely large.

In fact almost every game is bound to produce combinations, either in actual play or as possible continuations borne in mind by the players, but not actually appearing on the scene. This single consideration gives a good idea of the number of possible combinations as chess games normally do not repeat themselves apart from a few exceptions once every century or so. However, if one needs astronomic figures for calculating the number of possible combinations on the other hand, one can almost count up the ideas behind combinations on one's fingers.

In view of the fact that at the present moment there is no theory of combinations which is accepted by all chess specialists, I shall not try in this book to delimit the number of combinational ideas, as for this purpose very extensive research would be necessary to prove one's opinions. Therefore we shall merely examine in this chapter those ideas which occur most frequently in practice, but we shall not go deeply into details. The small scope of this book allows only a few examples to illustrate each idea, and moreover we shall use only textbook-type examples and positions from actual games. However (in the course of this development) the student must become familiar with concrete examples of how the same idea is realized by the sacrifice of various pieces with this or that resultant blow. With this end in view, I very strongly recommend the reader to compile a notebook containing a collection of combinational ideas. More will be said about this later, when we begin analyzing positions.

Combinations Based on Attracting

(Diagram No. 27. White to move)

One's first impression is that White must resign because of the threat 1...Nf3ch to which he has no satisfactory defense. True, there are two circumstances which create motifs for seeking a combination by White, namely the position of the Black king which has no move, and the fact that White has three pieces acting on his direction. All the same if one were to analyze the position without sufficient care these motifs would be rejected as inadequate if the player were not familiar with the idea of diversion. Once one is familiar with this idea it is quite easy to find mate in two by:

      1 Qg8ch! Kxg8
      2 Re8 mate

White's queen sacrifice attracts the king onto a bad square from where he has no escape from the back rank.

(See Diagram No. 28)

In this example we see an initial attracting sacrifice which sets up another one, two moves later.

      1 ...   Rh1ch!

Leaving White no choice.

      2 Kxh1   Qh7ch
      3 Kg1   Qh2ch!

This second attracting sacrifice draws the king into

range of a deadly discovered check.

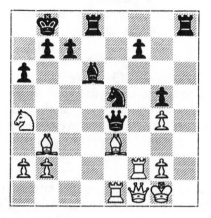

(Diagram No. 28. Komov vs. Sidorov, correspondence
1952. Black to move)

4	Kxh2	Nf3 dis. dbl. ch
5	Kh1	Rh8 mate

Here is another example of a diversionary sacrifice
leading to mate.

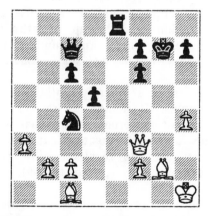

(Diagram No. 29. White to move)

1   Bh6ch   Kg6

Black refuses the sacrifice as after 1...Kxh6 there
follows 2 Qxf6ch Kh5 3 Qg5 or Bf3 mate. Retreating

the king to the back rank would also lead to mate.

2 h5ch

White thus forces acceptance of the bishop sacrifice and so diverts the king onto **h6**.

2 ... Kxh6
3 Qxf6ch Kxh5
4 Bf3 mate

In the three mating combinations which we have just seen the idea of diversion was carried out by sacrifices of queen, rook and bishop. However the same idea might be carried out in an appropriate position by sacrificing just a pawn.

We recommend the reader to compose text-book positions independently for himself in which mate is achieved by sacrifices with the idea of attracting some piece or pawn to some inferior square.

Next we shall consider an example where an attacking sacrifice is undertaken not for mate, but for the win of the queen and by means of a rook sacrifice. Any player who wishes to develop his combinational vision and fantasy ought to compile a whole set of positions in which various pieces are sacrificed for attracting purposes with the achievement of various advantages. In this way a collection is built up of attracting sacrifices, which is very useful. Then this should be done for all the remaining ideas which we shall consider later.

One must not stop at merely collecting a considerable number of examples. It stands to reason that the resultant blow can be of different sorts. That means that one should think up text-book positions in which double attacks of all sorts are the resultant blow (i.e. simple attacks, attacks exploiting pins, and so on).

Finally at the end of your notebook you should compile a large number of examples of combined ideas realized by the sacrifice of various pieces with various advantages for the active side.

The player who carries out the comprehensive task

that we recommend above will soon feel how much his playing strength has increased, and how much his combinational vision and imagination have developed.

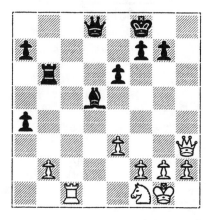

(Diagram No. 30. White to move)
>   **1 Rc8**

By pinning the queen with his rook White forces its capture which diverts the queen onto a bad square.

>   **1 ...   Qxc8**
>   **2 Qh8ch**

And wins the queen.

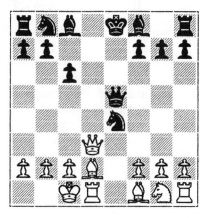

(Diagram No. 31. Reti vs. Tartakover, Vienna 1910. White to move)

It isn't easy to find the brilliant combination which Reti made. However, a knowledge of the idea of attracting and the great effect of a double attack and in particular of a double check definitely eases the process.

1 Qd8ch!!

The queen is sacrificed with the aim of attracting the king to **d8** where it is open to attack by a rook and bishop "battery".

1 ...	K x d 8
2 Bg5 dbl ch	Kc7

Or 2...Ke8 3 Rd8 mate.

3 Bd8 mate

In the next diagram, the position of White's queen and rook seems to "ask for" a fork - this is the motif for the combination.

(Diagram No. 32. Rudakovsky vs. Bondarevsky, XII USSR Ch 1940. Black to move)

1 ...	g 4 !

Black sacrifices a pawn so as to attract the queen to **g4**. As the pawn attacks both pieces and White cannot make sufficient counterplay he has to accept the sacrifice.

2 Qxg4	N e 5

The resultant blow, once again a double attack.

3 Qg2	N x f 3 c h
4 Qxf3	R f 7

As a result of the combination, Black has won the exchange for a pawn.

Blocking Combinations

In the positions we have examined above the resultant blow exploited the poor position of a piece attracted. Obviously when we speak about the poor position of a piece we are not referring to its isolation from the main scene of action, but merely the fact that in the position arising out of the sacrifice it is badly placed with regard to the actual piece position then obtaining. When we deal with *blocking*, attraction again takes place, but it is not the attracted piece that is exploited for the resultant blow, but another whose mobility has been restricted by the piece diverted.

We have already seen smothered mate. Let us consider next (next diagram) another combination with this aim, so as to become better acquainted with the idea of blocking.

(Diagram No. 33. White to move)

1 Nf7ch   Kg8
2 Nh6 dbl ch   Kh8
3 Qg8ch

The queen is sacrificed in order to divert the rook to **g8**. However, here, the resultant blow will be directed not at this rook, but at the king, which as a result of this diversion is deprived of his last possible move as **g8** is occupied, i.e. blocked.

    3 ...   **R x g 8**
    4 Nf7 mate.

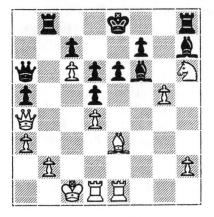

(Diagram No. 34. Baum vs O. Tahl, Leipzig 1975. Black to
move)

The White king is being "observed" by the **R b 8 a n d**
the **Bh7**. Nonetheless, it is not apparent how these
pieces could be put to work to make a successful raid on
White's king. But what if Black could play 1...**Qc4ch**
without having to fear **2 Qxc4?** Herein lies the answer.

    1 ...   **R b 4!**

Blocking the White queen's control of **c4**. Since neither **2 Qb3** n o r **2 Qc2** is possible because of loss of the
queen, White decides on **2 axb4** but then **2...Qc4ch**
forces either **3 Kd2 Qc2 mate** or **3 Qc2 Qxc2 mate.**

(See Diagram No. 35)

The legendary master of attack Tal deftly handles a
mating attack by using a brilliant blocking move.

    1 Qh6

Straightforward, so far. Both **2 Qxf8 mate** and **2 Qxf6**
m a t e are threatened.

    1 ...   **R x g 3**

But this seems to hold the position for Black since now
2 Qxf8ch is well met by **2...Rg8** and **2 Qxf6ch** allows
2...Rg7. But Tal has foreseen an elegant blocking move

which "short-circuits" Black's defense.

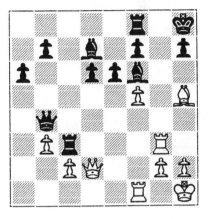

(Diagram No. 35. Tal vs. Platonov, Dubna 1974. White to move)

2 Bg6!!

A spectacular blow. Now **3 Qxf8 mate** is threatened again, but also a new mate at **h7**. Note the **Bg6** blocks the g-file to create the first threat.

2 ...   Rxg6

The only move since **2...fxg6** allows **3 Qxf8 mate.**

3 fxg6

Again mate at **f 8** and **h7** are threatened, and this time there is no way to delay the inevitable.

3 ...   fxg6
4 Qxf8 mate

(See Diagram No. 36)

White can go in for a sacrifice based on blocking.

1 Rxd5

Black cannot accept the sacrifice as after **1...exd5 2 Qxd5ch** his queen is diverted onto **f 7** after which White mates by **3 Rh8.** Hence the combination wins White a knight.

In practice a sacrifice with the idea of blocking occurs almost exclusively in mating combinations, to restrict a king's possible moves.

(Diagram No. 36. White to move)

The following combination which is to be found in a manuscript of the Italian player Greco dates from about 1625!

(Diagram No. 37. Black to move)

1	...	Nf2ch
2	Ke1	Nd3 dbl ch
3	Kd1	Qe1ch
4	Nxe1	Nf2 mate

Combinations Based on Diversion

The motif for seeking a combination in this particular case is a defending king position blocked in by its own unmoved pawns. This pawn position normally forms the best defensive covering for a king in the middlegame. However in those cases where there are open lines in the center or elsewhere along which the heavy pieces (queen, rook) act, one must be on one's guard, as penetration to the back rank by one of these pieces can lead to mate. This is why in such situations experienced players, when a convenient opportunity affords itself, make a so called outlet for the king in good time: they advance one of the pawns in front of the king. Normally it is best to advance a rook's pawn or knight's pawn one square, but of course other variations of this are quite possible.

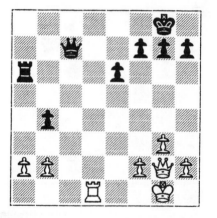

(Diagram No. 38. White to move)

In this position a suitable outlet would be created by Black's advancing his 'g' or 'h' pawn one square. Obviously there would then be no question of a back row mate. It stands to reason that the square to be used for the king's outlet must not be under attack itself. Thus if in Diagram 38 one adds a White bishop at b1, the 'g' pawn, by advancing to Black's third rank would then provide an outlet, whereas the 'h' pawn would not. In the actual position there is no outlet, which indicates a motif for a combination, and we begin to look for a means of penetrating to the eighth rank with queen or rook. A suitable square for this penetration is **d8** which is guarded only by the Black queen. The thought occurs - can't the Black queen be diverted so as to deprive it of its essential function? This search leads us to the move **1 Qb7!** Here the idea of diversion is realized by means of a double attack as both Black's queen and rook are attacked and Black cannot capture the queen because of his obligation to defend **d8**.

We have already said in the first chapter and can convince ourselves once again here that the most dangerous blows are the various forms of double attack since, as a rule, they greatly limit the opponent's replies or even deprive him of any satisfactory defense. So it is in Diagram 38 Black loses at once.

(Diagram No. 39. White to move)
White wins the queen by diverting the Black king from its defense by the rook sacrifice: **1 Rh7ch!**

(See **Diagram No. 40**)
In this example we see diversion used to set up a mating attack.
1 Nf6ch!
A forcing move inasmuch as this move forks both king and queen. The main idea is to divert the **Bg7** from its defense of **h6**. This in turn will allow a brisk mating attack.

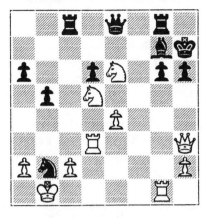

(Diagram No. 40. Chevaldonnet vs. Blanc, Val Thorens, 1977. White to move)

1	...	B x f 6
2	Qxh6ch!	

Drawing the king to a fatally exposed square.

2	...	K x h 6
3	Rh3ch	B h 4
4	Rxh4	mate

(Diagram No. 41. Nimzovitch vs. Marshall, New York 1927. White to move)

White's advantage is clear at the first glance, which suggests the search for a combination. The motifs here may be stated as the dangerous position of Black's king, the pin on the knight, and the fact that Black's rook and bishop have no direct part in the game, whereas White's pieces are superbly placed.

1 Re8!

The rook sacrifice diverts the Black queen from the defense of the knight.

    1 ...   Qxe8
    2 Qxf6ch   Kg8
    3 Bh6   Resigns

If **3...Qf7** then mate by **4 Qd8ch** and **5 Qxf8.**

(Diagram No. 42. Mikenas vs Bronstein, Tallin 1965. Black to move)

We observe here that with White's king tucked in the corner, it might be possible to play against White's first rank to create a mating threat. But the direct attempt **1...Qe1ch** expecting **2 Rxe1 Rxe1ch 3 Qf1 Rxf1 mate** is too optimistic. White would substitute **2 Qf1** for **2 Rxe1** thus maintaining a defense. Bronstein notices a subtle dependency in the position: the **Ra1** must keep guard on the first rank while the White 'b' pawn must shield the **Ra1** from the diagonal (e5-a1) action of the **Qe5.** This leads to Black's startling first move.

    1 ...   Rxa3!

Now **2 bxa3** allows **2...Qxa1ch** with mate after **3 Bd1 Re1ch 4 Qf1 Rxf1,** or **3 Qd1 Re1ch,** while **3 Rb1** or **3 Qb1** both lose to **3...Re1ch.** Another facet of this combination arises after **2 Qxa3**. Now that the reply **2 Qf1** is ruled out, our initially optimistic idea of **2...Qe1ch** now works after **3 Rxe1 Rxe1 mate.**

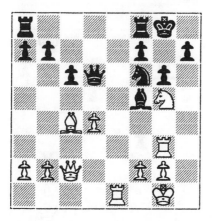

(Diagram No. 43. Kholmov vs Golz, Dresden 1956. White to move)

The concentration of White's pieces aiming at the kingside enables him to make a combination with the idea of diversion. After the initial sacrifice the awkward position of Black's queen plays a big part.

1 Qxf5!   gxf5

Obviously Black cannot play **1...Qxg3** because of **2 Qxf6**. This variation would be "desperado" play by Black's queen which is doomed anyway. Here the desperado doesn't work for Black, but all the same one should never fail to take account of such intermediate moves when analyzing, otherwise one could get a nasty surprise. We have already spoken about this in detail earlier in Chapter One. After Black's text move the White "battery" of rook and knight plays the decisive role.

2 Ne4 dis. ch

A double attack in two directions.

2 ...   Qxg3

It is essential to take this reply into account at the beginning of the combination. A king move out of check would simply leave him a piece down after **3 Nxd6**.

3 Nxf6ch

This is an "intermediate" move on White's part. If now 3...Kg7 then a new double attack, this time by one piece - 4 Nh5ch - would leave White with material advantage.

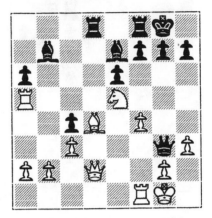

(Diagram No. 44. Bilek vs Stein, Kecskemet 1968. Black to move).

Here we see that Black's **B b 7** and **Q g3** focus on **g 2** with a potential mate threat there. Only White's **Qd2** is guarding g2; therefore we can seek any way to divert the White queen from its all-important guard duty.

1 ...   **R x d 4!**

Now **2 Qxd4** is impossible because then **g 2** is left unguarded.

2 cxd4   **Bb4!**

Winning a piece after **3...Bxa5,** since **3 Qxb4** allows mate.

(See Diagram No. 45)

This is a more complicated example. Black uses the diversion idea as the basis of a trap. In the game Black played:

1 ...   **B h 6**

Now White has to retreat his queen to **f2.** True, after **2 Qf2 Qxf2 3 Rxf2 e6** his game would be difficult; for example **4 Nf6ch Ke7 5 Nxd7 Be3** etc. White fell into a cunning trap and soon had to resign.

2 Rxh5

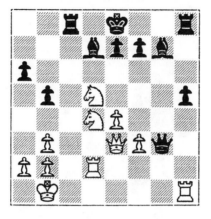

(Diagram No. 45. Boleslavsky vs Bondarevsky, Match Tournament 1941. Black to move)

White apparently supposed that his opponent had blundered and forgotten about his king shut in on the back rank: obviously the White queen cannot be captured, because of **3 Rxh8** mate. But it was the boxed-in position of the White king that Black planned to exploit when he laid the trap. For this purpose he tempted his opponent to capture the 'h' pawn so diverting his rook from the back rank.

2 ...   Rg8!

After this all becomes clear. Black sets up a double attack indirectly - he threatens to capture the queen and on top of that threatens a back row mate.

3 Qd3   Qg1ch!

White resigned, because of **4 Rd1 Rc1ch 5 Rxc1 Qxc1** mate.

Combinations Based on Square-Freeing

Sometimes positions arise in which a piece or pawn of the attacker's interferes with the action of another piece or pawn. Let us elucidate by a few examples.

(See Diagram No. 46)

In seeking out combinative chances, it is always a good idea to spot the opponent's unprotected pieces. In the given position, the **Ra3** being unprotected can be exploited by a sacrificial move paving the way for a square-freeing follow up.

(Diagram No. 46. Mikenas vs Polugaevsky, USSR 1966.
Black to move)

1 ...   Rxd3!
2 Bxd3   c 4

Clearing the c 5 square for the queen. Now if **3 Be2** then **3...Qc5ch** and **4...Qxa3** follows and Black has won a piece. However, White, seeing this, tries a clever move to exploit Black's back rank.

3 Qd6

A good try. Now if **3...cxd3** then **4 Qxc6** wins since **4...Rxc6** is impossible due to **5 Rb8ch** and mate in three.

3 ...   Ne8!

But this eliminates the back rank mates while "bumping" the queen.

4 Qb4

Other queen moves are no improvement.

4 ...   Qxb4
5 cxb4   c x d 3

The result is that Black has won two pieces for a rook with a powerful passed pawn at d3. If now **6 Rxd3** then **6...Bxa4** and Black has a won ending. Also if **6 b5** then **6...axb5 7 axb5 Bxb5! 8 Rxb5 d2!** wins (*9 Rd3 Rc1ch and 10...d1=Q*).

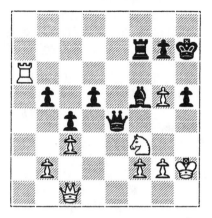

(Diagram No. 47. White to move)

White's **g 5** is occupied by a White pawn. If one were to remove it and place the White knight in its place, Black would be lost because of a double attack. Hence the thought arises of forcibly freeing this square by sacrificing the pawn.

1 g6ch   Bxg6

Refusal of the sacrifice would also lead to immediate loss.

2 Ng5ch

Etc.

(Diagram No. 48. Mirkin vs Sasin, USSR 1978. Black to

move)

Black has total domination on the e-file; with White's king immediately adjacent it is natural to seek out possibilities for attack. Black's first move creates a decisive pattern of attack.

                       1 ...   Rf1ch!

Now if **2 Qxf1** then **2...Qe3** is mate (*Note that Qxf1 removes a flight square for White's king*). Also if **2 Kxf1** then **2...Qe1** is mate.

                       2 Kg3

The only other choice.

                       2 ...   Qg5ch
                       3 Rg4   Re3ch

And White must give up his queen with **4 Qxe3** with an easy win for Black.

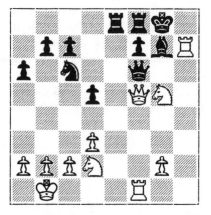

(Diagram No. 49. White to move)

White cannot capture twice on **f6** because he would be mated on the back rank. At the same time Black has an immediate mate threat on **b2** and another winning threat in **1...Qxf5**. What should White do? Can it really be that the dangerous position of Black's king attacked by three pieces is an inadequate motif for a combination? If one did not know of square-freeing one could easily overlook the combination, but once one has become familiar with this idea the winning

                       1 Rh8ch!

is found at once as mate follows on **h7**, just freed by

the rook sacrifice.

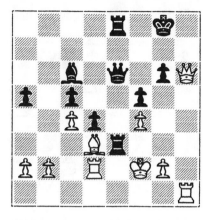

(Diagram No. 50. Kmoch vs Rubinstein, Semmering 1926.
Black to move)
White threatens mate by 1 **Qh8ch**, etc, and generally speaking his position looks quite satisfactory. However it is Black to move and White's king position is unsafe just like Black's. True it is not immediately apparent how Black can penetrate into his opponent's position despite his trebled major pieces on the e-file. Only the square freeing idea gives the solution to this problem.

1 ...   Rf3ch!

White resigned, as Black forces mate in all variations for all his moves are checking ones, and so have the greatest degree of compulsion. White's queen and rook actively placed on the h-file stand powerless witnesses of the king's downfall.

(See Diagram No. 51)

White's bishop and queen are poised on the **b1-h7** diagonal with ideas of delivering mate at **h7**. But the stalwart **Nf6** guards the square and there seems to be no way to remove its defensive function. Nonetheless, a square-freeing combination is available which will force checkmate.

1 Qh7ch

The idea is to clear the **g6** square for White's knights.

1 ...   N x h 7

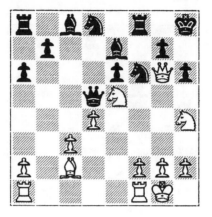

(Diagram No. 51. Kirilenko vs Maevskaja, USSR 1974.
White to move)

2 N4g6ch

But not 2 N5g6ch?? Kg8 3 Nxe7ch Kf7 and Black's
king escapes mate.

2 ...   Kg8
3 Nxe7ch Kh8
4 N5g6 mate

(Diagram No. 52. Flohr vs Byvshev, Semi-final XIX USSR
Ch 1951. White to move)

Black's queen defends the rook on his c7. If she were
attacked she would be embarrassed for a good move. Note

also that the queen guards the bishop so that it is "overloaded". White could advantageously attack the queen from c4, as then Black would not have any satisfactory defense. Hence we get the idea of freeing this square.

> 1 Bxf7ch! R x f 7
> 2 Rc4   Qd6

Otherwise comes 3 Qxc7.

> 3 Rxg4

By his combination White has won a pawn.

Line Freeing combinations

Having become familiar with square freeing now let us examine examples based on line freeing. It stands to reason that a knight, which has a special sort of jumping move, cannot benefit by line freeing. Similarly a pawn, which can only advance one square, can have no special line. For a pawn the concepts of square freeing and line freeing coincide. But an unmoved pawn has a "line" of movement, although it consists merely of two squares.

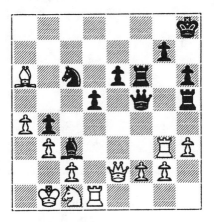

(Diagram No. 53. White to move)

> 1 Rxc3!   b x c 3
> 2 g4

The motif for the combination was the fact that Black's queen and rook were badly placed as if inviting a pawn fork. As a result White wins a piece for a pawn. In this case we have to free the square g 3 on which the rook stood. By sacrificing this rook for a bishop we free the line of action of the pawn, which passes through g3.

One could object that line freeing is unthinkable without also freeing a square. Obviously this is quite correct, but from a theoretical point of view, there is a difference and moreover - most important for our point of view- the division of the concepts of square freeing and line freeing is significant from the point of view of looking for a combination in practice.

Pay particular attention to the following position in which a type of line opening is carried out which is very common in practice, though obviously in a more complicated form. Incidentally, I have often been able to play such an elementary combination in simultaneous exhibitions.

(Diagram No. 54. White to move)

    1 Bxh7ch Kxh7

    2 Rxd7

Of course the player who makes a combination like this never thinks of it as freeing the square d3 so that the rook could come into action, rather his thoughts are taken up in looking for line freeing for the rook which is suggested by the motif of the unguarded Black rook on the d-file.

(Diagram No. 55. Alekhine vs Tartakover, Kecskemet
1927. White to move)

In the diagram White's combination repeats the idea
of line freeing by means of two sacrifices. The motif
suggesting the combination is the fact that Black's
queen is placed in the line of a "battery" consisting of
White's rook and bishop.

1   Nh6ch!

Freeing a line for the bishop on **d3**. Obviously the sacrifice must be accepted.

1 ...   h x g 6
2   Bxh7ch

The second line-freeing, this time for the rook. Black
accepted this second sacrifice, as its refusal also lost, e.g.
2...Kg7   3   Nf5ch and **4   Qxf7** or **4   Bxh6** mate; or
2...Kf8   3   Bxh6   mate or **2...Kh8   3   Qxf7   Nbd7**
(*3...Nfd7   4   Bg6* or *3...Rf8   4   Rxd8* or *3...Qc7   4   Nh5   Nxh5   5
Qxh5   Kxh7   6   Qxh6ch   Kg8   7   Qg6ch   Kh8   8   Rd5   with a decisive attack*) **4   Bf5** (*Alekhine gives   4   Nf5   with a mating
attack, but this is not so clear after   4...Bf8!   -   B.C.*) and
Black is quite helpless against White's various threats
such as **5   Bxd7   Nxd7   6   Nf5** or **5   Bxh6** or **5   Nh5.**

2 ...   N x h 7
3   Qg4ch

White could also win by **3   Rxd8   Bxc4   4   Rxe8ch   Bf8
5   Bf4** finishing up the exchange ahead. Alekhine
chooses an even simpler line.

| 3 ... | K h 8 |
| 4 Rxd8 | R x d 8 |

If **4...Bxd8** then **5 Qf3** again forcing **5...Nc6** giving up the knight. White has accurately calculated all the variations.

| 5 Qe4 | N c 6 |
| 6 Qxc6 | |

The combination has ended and White has a decisive material advantage.

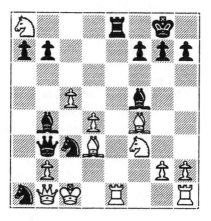

(Diagram No. 56. Druganov vs Panteleev, correspondence 1956. Black to move)

White's king is literally surrounded by a swarm of Black pieces, so it should come as no surprise that a decisive combination is at hand. In this case we shall see a sacrifice designed to clear a diagonal in order to effect mate.

| 1 ... | Qd1ch! |

A multi-purpose move which blocks a potential flight square at **d1** for White's king as well as clearing the **b 3** square for the **Na1**.

| 2 Rxd1 | Ne2ch! |

Illustrating the motif of line clearance - in this case the **f5-b1** diagonal is forced open.

| 3 Bxe2 | Nb3 mate |

Line Closing Combinations

This is the direct opposite of the previous section.

Whereas before we had sacrifices aiming at freeing or opening a line for the action of the active side's pieces, we now have the closing of the line of action of the defender's pieces by one of his own men.

(Diagram No. 57. White to move)
1 Nd6!

This wins the exchange, as after **1...cxd6** the Black queen's line of action is closed and White can play the forced maneuver **2 Nh6ch Kh8 3 Nxf7ch Kg8 4 Nxd6**. One could say that Black's unmoved 'c' pawn is attracted onto **d6** by the knight sacrifice, which means that we are dealing with the idea of attraction.

However a more careful analysis will convince us that the feature that is exploited is not the pawn on **d6**, but the closing of the queen's line of action.

With attraction it is the poor position of the attracted piece which is exploited; that is not the case here.

(See Diagram No. 58)
1 Rc6!

After this rook sacrifice, in the event of **1...Bxc6** the line of action of the forward rook is interrupted and **2 Qxc8 mate** follows.

If either rook captures on **c6** then the bishop's line is closed leading to mate by **2 Qb7**. Black has just one defense against mate: **1...Rb8**...but then **2 Rxc5** wins.

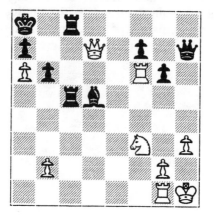

(Diagram No. 58. White to move)

(Diagram No. 59. Saemisch vs. Ahues, Hamburg 1946.
White to move)

White cannot play for mate by 1 f6 as Black has the reply 1...Qc5ch exchanging queens. Saemisch found a remarkable combination with the idea of line closing which occurs in two variations.

1 Re5!   Resigns

On 1...dxe5 closing the bishop's diagonal, mate follows at g7, whereas if 1...Bxe5 then 2 f6 and as the bishop has closed the fifth rank 2...Qc5ch no longer provides a defense against mate.

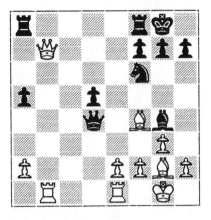

(Diagram No. 60. Stahlberg vs Persitz, Ljubljana 1955.
White to move)

In the following two combinations the idea is very close to the idea of line closing. The difference lies in the fact that the line of an opponent's piece is closed not by one of his own men but by a piece of the active side. It happens rarely in practice but one should be familiar with it.

Combinations Based on Isolation

Here the idea is realized in a very simple form (See Diagram No. 60).

1 Bb8!

If now **1...Rxb8 2 Qxb8** when the queen cannot be taken because of immediate mate. After **1 Bb8** the **Rf8** is shut out. This leads to the isolation of the other rook which is unguarded and has no safe square to which to go. Hence this simple combination wins the exchange.

Now let us examine a beautiful classic example from the play of the famous Czechoslovak Grandmaster Reti. This combination starts with a comparatively long forced maneuver. Apparently this is why M. Euwe in his book *Strategy and Tactics in Chess* assigned this combination to the category of "cumulative" combinations.

According to my theory this is a combination with an

introductory forced maneuver which is a component part of it.

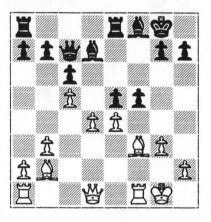

(Diagram No. 61. Reti vs. Bogolubov New York 1924. White to move)

1 Qc2

White threatens to capture not only on f 5 but also on e 5 as he has defended his 'c' pawn with his queen. What should Black do? To exchange on e 4 is disadvantageous as after **2 Bxe4** two pawns are *en prise*, both the 'e' pawn and the 'h' pawn. Black's answer is forced.

1 ...   exd4
2 exf5   Rad8

The counter-attack **2...Qe5** attacking the White pawns is unsatisfactory because of **3 Qc4ch Kh8 4 Bxd4 Qxf5 5 Bxc6** (*a line freeing combination, though a very simple one*). The attempt to attack the pawns with the rook also doesn't work - **2...Re5 3 Bxd4 Rxf5 4 Be4 Rxf1ch** (*4...Rh5 loses to 5 Qc4ch Kh8 6 Qf7 threatening the rook and mate on f8*) **5 Rxf1 h6** (*or 5...g6 6 Bxg6 etc.*) **6 Qc4ch Kh8 7 Qf7** with two decisive threats, **8 Qxf8ch** and **8 Qg6.**

3 Bh5   Re5

If the rook went to e 7 or e 3 then after **4 Bxd4** Black could not play **4...Bxf5** because of **5 Qxf5** when the bishop could not be captured because of mate on **f8.**

4 Bxd4   Rxf5
5 Rxf5   Bxf5

6 Qxf5   Rxd4

Black has maintained material equality, but if at the beginning of the forced maneuver he had seen the whole combination then he would surely have preferred to remain a pawn down to avoid what follows.

7 Rf1

White's pieces are concentrated for attack on the Black king. The introductory forced maneuver is coming to an end.

7 ...   Rd8

Obviously **7...Be7** loses to **8 Qf7ch**, etc. The defense **7...Qe7** is refuted by **8 Bf7ch Kh8 9 Bd5** (*isolating the Black rook so that it cannot return to d8*) **9...Qf6** (*there is nothing else*) **10 Qc8** and wins.

8 Bf7ch   Kh8

9 Be8!

The final move of the combination. Obviously the bishop cannot be captured because of mate. At the same time **9 Be8!** has isolated the Black major pieces which no longer act along the back rank to defend the bishop, so Bogolubov resigned.

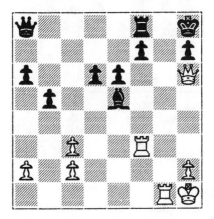

(Diagram No. 62. Soultanbeieff vs Borodin, Brussels 1943. White to move).

White would like to play **Qxh7ch** and on **...Kxh7** then **Rh3** with mate, but the **Qa8** pins the **Rf3** against the White king. But by noticing a subsidiary threat White can subtly break the Black lines of defense.

1 Rg2!!

This breaks the pinning action of the **Qa8**, hence activating the threat of **Qxh7ch** and **Rh3   mate**. The subsidiary threat follows **1...Qxf3** - it would allow **2 Qxf8 mate**. Nothing else works for Black either since **1...Rg8** also allows **2 Qxh7ch** and **3 Rh3 mate**.

Combinations Based on Destroying a Guard

In examining the ideas of attraction, diversion and so on, we have been dealing in essence with the removal of a defense in the wide sense of the word, as every combination pursues this aim. In the final analysis the defending side is deprived of all satisfactory defense and must lose material or suffer deterioration of his position. When speaking of combinations based on destroying the guard, we have in mind combinations in which the destruction takes place by means of a direct sacrifice; as one might put it, in its "crude form".

(Diagram No. 63. White to move)

Apparently Black has a sound position but by a simple exchange sacrifice White wins a piece.

1 Rxd6!

As in all our text book examples, this combination is of course quite elementary, but it gives a clear idea of what "destroying a guard" means. If the rook is captured there follows **2 Qxe7**. A sacrifice can be used not only to liquidate a piece or pawn which defends another man, but also to destroy the defense of some important point, as in the following example.

(Diagram 64. White to move)

The Black knight on **b6** is defending an important square as, if it were not for this knight, White would check on **d 7** and fork king and queen. Hence there arises the thought that if this knight were destroyed the defense of **d7** would be destroyed at the self same time.

1 Qxb6!

...and White wins at least a knight as, if **1...Qd5 2 Na6ch** and **3 Nxc7ch** finishing a rook up.

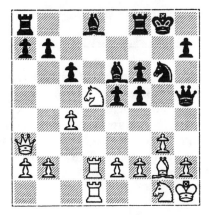

(Diagram No. 65. J. Rabinovich vs Panov, IX USSR Ch

1934. White to play)
1 Qd6
The introductory move to the combination.

    1 ...   Bf7

If 1...Bxd5 2 cxd5 with advantage as there is no satisfactory defense to the threat 3 dxc6.

2 Qxd8!

By sacrificing his queen White destroys the guard of
Black's f6. If either 2...Rxd8 3 Nxf6ch is the resultant
blow.

    2 ...   cxd5

If 2...Bxd5 then 3 Bxd5ch and if 3...Kh8 4 Bf3.

3 Qxf6

Assessing the final position we can say that White has
a definite advantage - he is a pawn up and if 3...dxc4
then 4 Rd7 is very unpleasant for Black.

(Diagram No. 66. Grigoryev vs Chistyakov, Moscow 1935.
Black to move)

White's king is badly placed. An attack along the open
h-file suggests itself. Examining this position carefully
we see that White's defense is based on his h3 square.
How can this be overcome? The square is defended by
both rook and knight. Can't one destroy one of the defending pieces by a sacrifice?

Analyzing all these factors we arrive at the analysis
of a queen sacrifice for White's knight. Exact analysis

shows that this combination is advantageous.

```
1 ...        Q x g 5
2 fxg5       R h 8 c h
3 Rh3        R x h 3 c h
4 gxh3       c5 dis ch
```

And mate next move.

(Diagram No. 67. Naranja vs Gheorghiu, Manila 1974.
Black to move)

In this position Black sets up a removal of the guard by preliminary exchanges.

```
1 ...        B x e 3
2 Qxe3
```

Now conditions have been set for a removal of the guard - the queen on e 3 will be the target of this operation.

```
2 ...        b x c 4 c h
3 Rxc4
```

No better would be 3 bxc4 because of 3...Rb3ch 4 axb3 Rxb3ch 5 Rc3 Rxc3ch 6 Kxc3 Qxe3ch winning material.

```
3 ...        R x b 3 c h
```

The same theme as in the previous note - the defender of the queen, the Nd3, is to be driven away, or subjected to an "x-ray" attack, leaving the Qe3 in the lurch.

```
4 axb3       R x b 3 c h
```

And Black wins after 5 Rc3 Rxc3ch as in the above note to 3 Rxc4.

Combinations Based on Seizing a Point

The actual name of the idea - seizing a vital point - gives a good idea of the theme of such combinations.

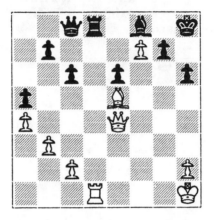

(Diagram No. 68. Nimzovich vs Rubinstein, Berlin 1928. White to move)

The Black king is badly placed and his main pieces - the queen and rook - play no part in his defense. **1 Qg6** suggests itself with the decisive threat of **2 Qxh6 mate**, but this involves giving up a rook.

Let us do the necessary calculation. **1 Qg6 Rxd1ch 2 Kg2 Rd2ch** (*mate could also be averted by 2...Rg1ch but after 3 Kxg1 Bc5ch 4 Kg2 there is no further defense*) **3 Kh3** and here too Black is defenseless. What was the idea of this combination?

Here we see neither attraction nor diversion nor any other idea that we have examined so far. We have something new here. The point of the combination is the seizure of a square, the occupation of which justifies the sacrifice.

(See Diagram No. 69)

Here too the Black king is in a difficult position. The drawbacks of a seriously weakened pawn formation are aggravated by the superb position of the White knight, for it only needs the White queen to penetrate to the kingside and it's all over. We have hardly thought about this before we immediately get the idea of seizing a square by means of the combination.

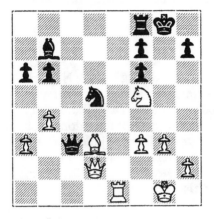

(Diagram No. 69. Spielmann vs Tartakover, Marienbad
1925. White to move)

    1 Qh6!   **Qxe1ch**
    2 Bf1

Now Black has no defense against mate.

(Diagram No. 70. Taimanov vs Zhukhovitsky, Semi-final
XVII USSR Ch 1949. White to move)

In this position Taimanov carelessly played **1 Ne6**, reckoning that the game was all over. However he fell into a cunning trap based on the idea of seizing a point.

$$1 \quad ... \quad Ng4$$

For seizing this square, no price can be too high! There are two threats, 2...Qxh2 **mate**, and 2...Nf2 **mate**.

$$2 \quad g3$$

The only move.

$$2 \quad ... \quad Qc6ch$$
$$3 \quad Rg2 \quad Nf2ch$$

And Black wins. In all three examples we have shown sacrifices aimed at seizing a point, which led to mate or a quick win. Naturally combinations for seizing a point can lead to the most diverse kinds of advantage. As in all combinations, the sacrifice needs only to be justified by subsequent achievements. The following classic example illustrates this very well.

(Diagram No. 71. Torre vs Lasker, Moscow 1925. White to move)

The inadequately defended Black king position and the activity of the White pieces on the king's side serve as weighty motifs for undertaking a combination. It is interesting that such an outstanding player as Emanuel Lasker, world champion for 27 years, paid inadequate attention to these motifs.

$$1 \quad Bf6!$$

A queen sacrifice with the idea of seizing the point g7.

$$1 \quad ... \quad Qxh5$$

Now White plays a forced maneuver which it has become customary to call the "treadmill". I advise the reader to make a note of this manuever.

2 R x g 7 c h   K h 8
3 R x f 7 dis ch K g 8
4 R g 7 c h   K h 8
5 R x b 7 dis ch K g 8
6 R g 7 c h   K h 8
7 R g 5 c h

The White rook has destroyed almost all the 7th rank. He refrains from capturing the 'a' pawn by a continuation of the process so as not to open a file for the Black rook along which the rook could capture White's 'a' pawn and so become active after the end of the combination.

7 ...   K h 7
8 R x h 5   K g 6

This double attack by his king wins back a piece, but he remains three pawns down.

9 R h 3   K x f 6
1 0 R x h 6 c h

Destroying Combinations

If a combination is directed against a certain target and is accompanied by sacrifices so as to make this target open to subsequent attack, we say that a destroying combination has been carried out. In order to expose the target to attack, that is to destroy the greater part of its protective cover of pieces and pawns, considerable sacrifices may be called for, with no half measures. Hence the question immediately arises - is it all worth it?

If in actual fact the target of the combination is finally achieved, have the sacrifices been justified or have they been too great? Suppose the combination wins the opposing queen for the expenditure of less material. The "destroying" combination would be justified. When we open up a queen's position by means of sacrifices however, we tend to increase its mobility, and it is practically impossible to win an "open" queen. The same considerations apply to a rook and for an "open" rook one can sacrifice only a minor piece, otherwise the combination would be pointless.

But can one really achieve much destruction by
means of a minor piece sacrifice only? All these general
considerations are mentioned in order to explain why in
practical play, destroying combinations are normally
confined to operations against the king. In order to
"win" the king, i.e. to mate him, one can of course go in
for the greatest possible sacrifices. Moreover the king is
not only a piece of little mobility, but is subject to particular rules which restrict his movements even more.
Of course it is not essential that a destroying combination should end in mate. For a king to be exposed on an
open board in the middlegame is so dangerous that, to
save himself from the harassment of the attacking
pieces, a defender may be forced to surrender a lot of
material which generally makes a combination sound
even if it doesn't force mate, as the material sacrificed
may be regained with interest. Let us examine a number
of examples from practical play: in the course of this we
shall make some supplementary remarks about destroying combinations of types often encountered in practice.

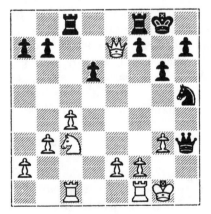

(Diagram No. 72. Bannik vs Tal, Semi-final XXIII USSR Ch
1955. Black to move)

Having studied the position carefully we notice that
the White king's pawn protection has been weakened

and that there are no pieces at all to defend him. The Black queen and knight are menacingly near to him. These motifs suggest the direction of the main blow - the destruction of the White king's position.

	1 ...	N x g 3
	2 fxg3	Q x g 3 c h
	3 Kh1	

The destruction idea has been carried out by the sacrifice of knight for two pawns. The king is now completely open, but Black cannot win with his queen alone, so he has the new problem of bringing up his reserves as quickly as possible for a decisive attack on the king. If he goes about this too slowly, White's pieces will take up the protection of their king. Notice how, once the destruction has been carried out, Black adopts a carefully calculated plan for harassing the White king.

	3 ...	R c e 8
	4 Qxb7	

White captures the pawn so as to be able to return to g 2 for the defense. If instead 4 Qf6 then 4...Re5 5 Qf3 Qh4ch 6 Kg1 Rg5ch when White must give queen for rook. In this, note that Black must not play 5...Rh5ch for White would win by a diversion combination: 6 Qxh5 gxh5 7 Rg1. The possibility of this counter-combination reminds us yet again how careful we have to be in our analysis, remembering that even in a completely won position, a single careless move can immediately create a motif for a counter-combination.

	4 ...	R e 5
	5 Qg2	R h 5 c h
	6 Kg1	Q e 3 c h
	7 Qf2	

Obviously White's last few moves have been forced; 7 Rf2? Rg5.

	7 ...	Q h 6

Now there are threats of both 8...Rh1ch 9 Kg2 Qh3 m a t e and 8...Rg5ch.

	8 Qxa7	

Freeing f2 for the king's flight.

	8 ...	Q g 5 c h
	9 Kf2	R h 2 c h
	10 Ke1	

If **10 Kf3** then **10...Rh3ch 11 Ke4** (*11 Kf2 Qg3 mate*) **11...Qe5** mate. By occupying **e 1** the White king has blocked a line.

| 10 ... | Qxc1ch |
| 11 Nd1 | |

The forced operation begun by the knight sacrifice is now finished. Black is the exchange up in a fine position.

What did we see in this example? There were sacrifices; forced maneuvers including one with the idea of line closing. However the sacrifices were played by Black without exploiting any of the tactical ideas that we have studied so far. The whole combination represents a definite plan and has a strategical nature. Of course in destroying combinations one can have as component parts combinations with various tactical ideas but everything is basically subordinated to the idea of destruction followed by an attack on the exposed king. One can hardly say that Tal's combination consisted of attracting the White king to **h 1** and leave it at that. This assertion seems to me to be quite naive. The essential point, as we have seen, was not the attraction of the king to **h1**, but the stripping of the king's pawn cover when Black had an accurately calculated plan of exploiting the resulting exposed situation of the king. It is just as incorrect to speak merely of destroying the guard; in this case it is the guarding piece or pawn that is destroyed, and not just the pawn cover of the king.

(See Diagram No. 73)

The Black king is not yet castled while White is fully developed. This state of affairs serves as a clear motif for attacking the Black king. But how? The idea of a combination for destruction immediately occurs to us.

Concrete analysis shows that there is a combination with a queen sacrifice.

| 1 exf6 | Qxc2 |

Acceptance is forced as, if **1...Qxh4** then simply **2 fxg7 Rg8 3 f6** with a simple win- **3...Nxf6** is then impossible because of **4 Qf5.**

| 2 fxg7 | Rg8 |

(Diagram No. 73. Lilienthal vs Capablanca, Hastings
1934-5. White to move)

3 Nd4

White has destroyed the Black king position by his
queen sacrifice, completely opening it up for attack.
Notice that the king has not a single move and that the
activity of White's bishop and knight has greatly increased. Apart from that, one of the White rooks is about
to start work on the king's file. All this a logical conse-
quence of the opening up of the position. Along with
this, as we already said at the beginning of the section,
the power of the pieces grows and the king is in a very
dangerous situation. In stopping mate Black is already
forced to suffer great material loss, so White finishes
better off.

3 ...	Qe4

If 3...Qxc3 4 Rae1ch Ne5 5 Rxe5ch Kd7 6 Re7ch
and White wins.

4 Rae1	Nc5
5 Rxe4ch	Nxe4
6 Re1	

White now picks up the knight and is material to the
good with a much better position.

In this example we saw an exactly calculated plan of
attack after the sacrifice, whereby the king position
was destroyed. In this particular case the sacrifice is not

direct but indirect, as it is not the queen but the 'e'
pawn that, at the price of the queen, brings about the
destruction, but this is a detail which has no significance in principle. The strategical nature of the combination is, again, clear. It is not a case of attracting the
king; the analogy of this with the immediately preceding examples is obvious.

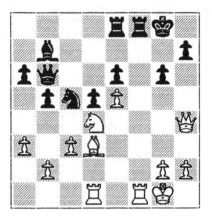

(Diagram No. 74. Bialas vs Stahlberg, Hamburg 1955.
White to move)

Once again we have a weakened castled position and
pieces distant from the defense of the kingside. The
same motifs and again a destroying combination.

1 Bxg6   h x g 6

By sacrificing the bishop, White aims to strip the king
of pawn cover as in the Bannik vs Tal game. Here however the drawback of the open king position is exploited, as we shall see, along with another minus in the
Black position.

2 Qh6

White threatens to play **3 Qxg6ch Kh8 4 Rf6**, after
which Black would have no defense. For example, if
4...Rxf6 5 exf6 threatening both **6 Qg7 mate** and **6
Qxe8;** or if **4...Qc7 5 Qh6ch.**

2 ...   Qc7

Bringing up the queen for defense. If instead **2...Ne4**
then White could play **3 Rxf8ch Rxf8 4 Qxg6ch Kh8
5 Rd3.**

3 b4

White drives the knight away so as to deprive the 'e' pawn of defense. If **3...Ne4** White could play this combination with the idea of attraction: **4 Rxf8ch Rxf8 5 Qxf8ch Kxf8 6 Nxe6ch**; the resultant blow is a fork, and after **6...Ke7 7 Nxc7 Nxc3 8 Rd3 d4 9 Rh3** (*not 9 Rxd4 Ne2ch*) when White wins. A more stubborn defense is **3...Qxe5** although White's advantage is clear in this case too: **4 Rxf8ch Rxf8 5 Qxg6ch Kh8** (*or 5...Qg7 6 Qxg7ch and 7 bxc5*) **6 Qh6ch Kg8 7 bxc5** with an extra pawn and the better position.

$$\begin{array}{lll} 3 & ... & Qg7 \\ 4 & Rxf8ch & Rxf8 \\ 5 & Qxg7ch & Kxg7 \\ 6 & bxc5 \end{array}$$

White is a pawn up and has a positional advantage.

Comparing this example with the previous ones we notice that in this case a second combination, based on diversion, formed a component part of the combination, but the basic aim remained - destruction.

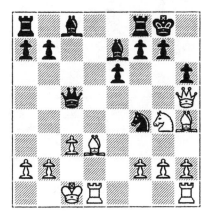

(Diagram No. 75. Bondarevsky vs Zagoryansky, Semi-final XIV USSR Ch 1944. White to move)

Exploiting his piece concentration on the king's side, White carries out a destroying combination.

1 Nxh6ch

The combination beginning **1 Nf6ch** works only in

two variations, i. e. **1...Bxf6 2 Qxc5** or **1...gxf6 2 Qxh6** but by playing **1...Kh8** Black could still defend.

        1 ...   **g x h 6**

If **1...Kh8 2 Nxf7ch Kg8 3 Bh7** mate.

        2 Qxh6   **N g 6**

    2...f5 was hopeless for Black because of **3 Bxe7 Qxe7** - **3...Nxd3ch 4 Rxd3** is worse - **4 Qxf4** with two pawns up (*and if 2...Nxd3ch 3 Rxd3 Bxh4 4 Rg3ch Bxg3 5 hxg3 - the same winning idea as in the main line*).

        3 B x g 6   **f x g 6**
        4 Q x g 6 c h   **K h 8**
        5 Q h 6 c h   **K g 8**
        6 R d 3   **B x h 4**

Other moves too would not have prevented a quick win by White.

        7 Q g 6 c h   **K h 8**
        8 R g 3 !

The simplest line. Black resigns.

(Diagram No. 76. van Hoorde vs Fichtl, Ghent 1954. Black to move)

White's king position has a good pawn cover, but the circumstances that there are no defending pieces on this side allows Black to go in for a combination whose main idea once again is destruction.

        1 ...   **B x h 2 c h !**
        2 K x h 2   **Q h 6 c h**

At first sight this may look like a combination based

on attraction. In fact Black's bishop sacrifice has attracted the king onto **h2**, so that a double attack on king and knight follows. However we shall soon see this conclusion to be a superficial one.

3 Kg1	**N x d 2**

Of course not **3...Qxd2 4 Bxe4.**

4 Bc1	

This reply wins the Black knight. If we had a simple case of an attractive combination, it would have been an incorrect combination. But Black has calculated everything accurately and it will soon be apparent that his intention was a destruction combination. Hence it was objectively better for White to play **4 Rfe1.**

4 ...	**Nf3ch!**

A new sacrifice for diversion whereby Black achieves a significant destruction of White's castled position, which he had already envisaged when playing the first move of his combination.

5 gxf3	**Qh3**

Now the king is open to frontal attack for which purpose Black will bring his rook into play via **f6**.

6 Bf4	

If **6 f4** then **6...Qg4ch** and **7...Rf6**. White has no satisfactory defense.

6 ...	**R f 6**
7 Bg5	

If White moves his rook from **f1** then Black continues by **7...Rg6ch 8 Bg3 Rh6.**

8 f4	**h 6**

Black now wins back the piece and remains material up.

(See Diagram No. 77)

Black's queen, two bishops and knight are aimed at White's kingside, while the White pieces hardly take any part in the defense of the king. All this adds up to motifs for a destruction combination.

1	...	**B x h 3**
2	**g x h 3**	**Q x h 3 c h**
3	**K g 1**	**B h 2 c h**
4	**K h 1**	**N f 4 !**
5	**N x f 4**	**B x f 4 c h**

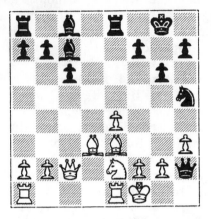

(Diagram No. 77. Davidson vs Alekhine, Semmering 1926.
Black to move)

6	Kg1	Bh2ch
7	Kh1	Qf3ch

A combination based on attraction.

8	Kxh2	Re5

This is the standard maneuver for creating decisive threats with which we have already become familiar.

9 Qc5

There is no other move.

9	...	Rxc5
10	Bxc5	Qh5ch
11	Kg2	Qxc5

Black has a decisive material advantage.

We have quoted a number of examples from practical play in all of which the active side gained an advantage by means of a combination for destruction. One must also note in particular that such a destroying combination often occurs in cases where one side, finding himself in a difficult position, goes in for a combination to get a draw by perpetual check. It can be quite logical for a combination to aim at a draw, based on an exposed king's position.

It may be quite difficult to classify a combination on the basis of the ideas incorporated in it. Chess is so complicated that in practice it is a common occurrence to see combinations in which quite a variety of tactical ideas are interwoven to form a unified whole. Often when dealing with such a union of ideas it is difficult to allot to any one of them the principal role. We shall now consider some examples of this sort, deliberately choosing the simplest examples. One must also remark that it is not always possible to establish a clear boundary between two different ideas.

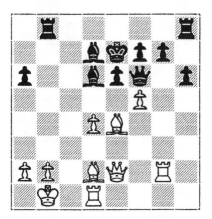

(Diagram No. 78. Portisch vs Florian, Budapest 1955.
Black to move)

1 ...	R x b 2 c h
2 Kxb2	Qxd4ch
3 Bc3	Rb8ch and wins

All this is clear and simple from the practical point of view. But just try to state what the idea of the combination was. One could talk about both destruction and also attraction of the king. Thus there are cases where it is impossible to classify everything exactly. Take another example.

(See Diagram No. 79)

White mates in two by 1 Rxh7ch and 2 Qh5. What was the idea of the combination? As a result of the sacrifice the king was attracted to h7 but this is also a case of destruction. In general one could put it that in view of the minimal destruction of the king's position the ideas of destruction and attraction merge.

(Diagram No. 79. White to move)

Combinations with Blended Motifs

(Diagram No. 80. Gerasimov vs Smyslov, Moscow 1935.
Black to move)

As we have already seen, a concentration of pieces aiming at the opposing king may be a good motif for a combination.

> **1 ...   Rd3!**

The rook puts himself *en prise* to two pieces. If **2 Bxd3** then the bishop is diverted from the defense of **g2** and

White is mated on that square. After **2 Qxd3** the queen is attracted onto a poor square which is exploited by **2...Bh2ch 3 Kh1 Nxf2ch 4 Kxh2 Nxd3**. Hence the rook sacrifice has two ideas - attraction and diversion.

2   Qxb6

Other relies were no better, as becomes clear from the subsequent play.

2 ...   R x h 3

Once again a sacrifice with the idea of diversion. There is now a threat of **2...Qxb6 3 Nxb6 Bh2ch 4 Kh1 Nxf2** mate and if **3 Qxc6** then straight away **3... B h 2 c h** and **4...Nxf2 mate.**

3   Bd4

White defends his **f 2** but now follows the maneuver we saw in the Torre-Lasker game. In this case the "treadmill" is set up by a rook and a bishop, but they have exchanged roles.

3 ...   B h 2 c h
4   Kh1   B x e 5 c h
5   Resigns

On **5 Kg1** there follows **5...Bh2ch 6 Kh1 Bc7ch** winning the queen. In this example we have seen a combination of attraction and diversion, and not for the first time either - this is no accidental choice of example, as such a combination of attraction and diversion is often met with in practical play.

In the following example the awkward position of the White queen and rook allows Black to play a combination with ideas of diversion, attraction and line freeing.

(See Diagram No. 81)
1 ...   N f 3 c h
2   gxf3

The queen could not take because it would be diverted from the defense of the rook. Now however a diagonal has been freed for the Black queen and a simple exchange attracts the rook onto **f4** where it is lost.

2 ...   Q x f 4
3   Rxf4   g 5
4   Rxf5   e x f 5
6   Bxf5

White has two pawns for the exchange, but his king's

side pawns are broken up. Black's active position after
6...Rd2 makes his advantage clear.

(Diagram No. 81. Simagin vs Byshev, Lugansk 1955.
Black to move)

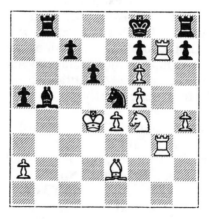

(Diagram No. 82. Savcenko vs Aleksej Ivanov, Vienna
1991. White to move).

Even though the queens are off the board the concentrated mass of White's pieces and pawns are up to the task of creating vigorous tactics.

1   Rxf7ch!

Destroying the **f7** pawn weakens the **e6** square, allowing the **Nf4** to jump into the thick of things.

1 ...   N x f 7

Alternatives are not satisfactory: 1...Kxf7 2 **Rg7ch**
Kxf6 3 **Nh5** mate; or 2...**Ke8** 3 **Re7ch Kd8** 4 **Ne6ch**
Kc8 5 **Rxc7** mate. If 3...**Kf8** (*instead of 3...Kd8*) then 4
N e 6 c h is mate; also if 1...**Kxf7** 2 **Rg7ch Kf8** then 3
Ne6ch   Ke8 and 4 **Re7** is mate.

2 N e 6 c h   K e 8
3 B x b 5 c h

Forcibly setting up a winning knight fork.

3 ...   R x b 5
4 N x c 7 c h   K d 7
5 N x b 5   R b 8
6 a 4

And White has an easily won position.

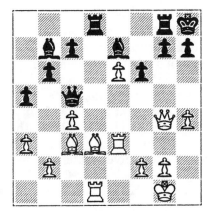

(Diagram No. 83. Duz-Khotimirsky vs Rotlevi, Carlsbad
1911. White to move.

1 B x h 7 !   R x d 1 c h
2 Q x d 1   R d 8

If Black were to capture the bishop then by 3 **Re5**
White would achieve a line-closing of the Black queen's
action from **h 5** and on 3...**fxe5** would come 4 **Qh5**
mate.

3 Bd3

White has won an important pawn and seriously
weakened Black's king position.

(Diagram No. 84. Kotov vs Bondarevsky, Leningrad 1936.
Black to move)

White is a rook up, but his king is badly placed. This
sets up the conditions for a combination by Black.

1 ...	f4ch!

Diverting the knight from the defense of f2.

2 Nxf4	Qf2ch
3 Kd3	Qxd4ch

Attracting the king even further into the center
where the minor pieces give mate.

4 Kxd4	Bc5ch
5 Kd3	Nxe5 mate

(See Diagram No. 85)

1 Rxd4!	

Destroying the defense of Black's f6. Black has to accept, as 1...Rxd5 2 Rxd5 Qxd5 would lead to the loss of
the queen after the line freeing 3 Nh6ch.

1 ...	cxd4
2 Nf6ch!	

Diverting the 'g' pawn so that if 2...gxf6 3 Qh6
forces mate.

2 ...	Kf8
3 Qxh7	

Now because of the threat 4 Qxg7 mate Black must
take the knight.

3 ...	gxf6

(Diagram No. 85. Duz-Khotimirsky vs Bannik, Semi-final XVII USSR Ch 1949. White to move)

4 Re1

A typical move in such positions. White prevents the escape of the king via **e8**. Now there is no defense against **5 Qg7 mate** and Black resigned.

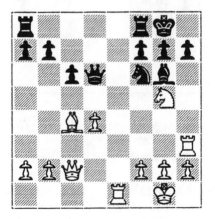

(Diagram No. 86. White to move)

This position can arise from a variation of the Queen's Gambit Declined. Black's castled position is sound, and defended by pieces, but all the same the concentration of White pieces against the king's side is quite considerable, sufficient to permit a combination.

1 Qxg6

The point of the queen sacrifice is to destroy the defender of f7, i.e. the bishop, and to divert the 'h' pawn from the rook's file, along which the White rook is acting.

1 ...   h x g 6
2 Bxf7ch! Rxf7

Now the rook is attracted on to f7, which as we shall see is bad for Black.

3 Rh8ch!

Yet another sacrifice. The rook attracts the king to h8 and simultaneously diverts him from the defense of the rook.

3 ...   K x h 8
4 N x f 7 c h

The resultant double attack "picking up" rook and queen. As a result of the combination White finishes a pawn up.

(Diagram No.87. Zagrebelnyj vs Ponyi, Magyarorszag 1992. White to move)

With both White's bishops and the N e 5 directed at the Black kingside, combinations are in the air.

1 Nxf7!!

Attracting the king to f7 and preparing to blast open the c4-f7 diagonal.

1 ...   K x f 7
2 d5!

Now if **2...Kg8** then **3 dxe6** threatening the **Qd8** is crushing, e.g. **3...Qe7 4 Rd7** traps the queen, while **3...Qc8** is met by **4 Qf3!** and Black is defenseless. Also, after **2...Qc8 3 dxe6ch Rxe6** (*3...Ke7 4 Rd7ch*) White continues **4 Qxe6ch! Qxe6 5 Rd7ch Ne7** (*5...Be7 loses the same way*) **6 Bxe6ch Kxe6 7 Rxb7** and White is the exchange and a pawn ahead with an easy win.

$$\text{2 ...} \qquad \text{exd5}$$
$$\text{3 Rxd5!}$$

The power of the discovered check comes into play.

$$\text{3 ...} \qquad \text{Rxe2}$$

There is nothing better.

$$\text{4 Re5 dis ch}$$

And it's mate after **4...Qd5 5 Bxd5.**

(Diagram No. 88. Tchigorin vs Davydov, St. Petersburg 1874. White to move)

Black is a rook up but his king position is open and his **Ra8** out of play. These are the basic motifs for Tchigorin's fine combination, but other defects of Black's position are also exploited, notably the placing of his queen and bishop.

$$\text{1 Qd4ch} \qquad \text{Kc8}$$

1...Nd5 is a better defense, hoping for **2 Bxd5 Qg3 ch 3 Bg2ch Qd6** with a tenable ending after **4 Qxd6ch cxd6 5 Nxe8 Kxe8 6 Bxb7 Rb8 7 Bc6ch Ke7.** However White plays **2 Qxd5ch Ke7** (*or 2...Kc8 3 Nxe8 Qg3ch 4 Qg2 Qe3ch 5 Rf2! Bh3! 6 Qf3 and White remains a* *piece up*) 3 Qxf7ch - B.C.

          2 Be6ch!

Now if **2...Bxe6** then the bishop is attracted away, so that the queen is lost, whilst if **2...fxe6** the bishops' diagonal is closed and White mates by **3 Qd7ch Kb8 4 Qxe8ch Nc8 5 Nd7** mate.

2	...	Kb8
3	Nd7ch	Kc8
4	Nc5ch	Kb8
5	Na6ch	

A fresh diversion!

5	...	bxa6
6	Qb4	mate

(Diagram No. 89. Adams vs Torre, New Orleans 1921.
White to move)

In this classic example the diversion is carried out several times with surprising beauty. The motif for the combination is the boxed-in position of the Black king, lacking a bolt-hole such as we have encountered before.

          1 Qg4!

Black's queen is diverted by this sacrifice from defending the **Re8**. Black replies with the only move which avoids immediate loss; if **1...Qxg4 2 Rxe8ch** mates.

1	...	Qb5
2	Qc4!	

This fine stroke diverts not only the queen but also

the **Rc8**. Once again Black plays his only move.

2 ...   Qd7

3 Qc7!

Yet another superb stroke.

3 ...   Qb5

Playing the queen one square further along the diagonal would shorten White's combination by one move as we shall soon see.

4 a4!

By this pawn sacrifice White attracts the queen onto a4. He could not play 4 Qxb7 straight away because of 4...Qxe2 when Black wins as, if then 5 Rxe2 Black mates in two by 5...Rc1ch while 5 Qxc8 loses a rook to 5...Qxe1ch 6 Nxe1 Rxc8.

4 ...   Qxa4

Now 4...Qxe2 is no good as after 5 Rxe2 there is no rook check on c1.

5 Re4!

This is why the Black queen was attracted on to a4. White's threat now is not 6 Rxa4, when Black would reply 6...Rxe1ch followed by 7...Rxc7, but 6 Qxc8 and if 6...Qxe4 7 Qxe8ch etc. Because of this threat of 6 Qxc8 Black hasn't time to make an outlet for his king, and must play the queen back to b5. But in the meantime White has moved his rook from e2 to e4 which gives him the chance to play the final wining stroke, once again based on diversion.

5 ...   Qb5

6 Qxb7!

Now Black doesn't have the chance of capturing on White's e2 which he would have if the rook had not got onto e4 by means of his attracting pawn sacrifice at move 4. Black has no defense and resigned.

In closing this chapter on combinative ideas, we draw attention once again to the necessity of working systematically at the development of combinational vision.

Apart from compiling a notebook of examples showing combinations according to their different ideas we also recommend the following: in our chess literature, tournament books, and various bulletins, many games can be found containing rich combinative play. You should select from these games positions in which combinations occurred and draw up diagrams showing the position in which the combination was begun, just as in this book. Then each time set up the position on the board and mentally work out, without moving the pieces, the combination in all its variations.

(*Bondarevsky is right in drawing attention to Soviet chess literature, as the best published compilations of positions for solving have undoubtedly been those appearing in Russian, notably Lisitsin's "Strategiya i Taktika Shakhmat" Moscow, 1958 - 542 pages, 1,326 diagrams! However, such collections are available in English, German and so on. In particular one can recommend the regular "Winning Practice" feature in the magazine "Chess", whose principal merit lies in the fact that the examples are generally up to date instead of repeating well known positions from the past - B.C*)

If at first it is difficult to find the solution there is no need to lose heart. Success doesn't come all at once. At first one can move the pieces about on the board in order to study the combination. Later when some experience has been gained it is essential to find the combination mentally and work out all the variations and possible defenses without moving the pieces. Even better is to write down the complete set of variations (once again without moving the pieces) so that the whole combination becomes even clearer.

When a large number of diagrams has been collected one can make a card-index file in which positions are divided according to their motifs, and, inside each division, subdivided according to their combinational ideas.

CHAPTER III

SACRIFICES

Once we have examined the various sorts of combinations we must devote particular consideration to yet another important middlegame question. This chapter will deal with sacrifices. Here the reader might well ask what sort of sacrifices we have in mind, in view of the fact that sacrifices have entered into every example in the book so far.

However a separate section on sacrifices is fully justified. The point is that in combinations the sacrifices are always accompanied by forced maneuvers as a result of which the active side gains an objective advantage. Hence the sacrifices we have considered were in essence temporary ones; analysis definitely established that after a certain number of moves either the opponent would be mated or the sacrificed material would be won back. Hence the sacrifice was not a sacrifice in the full sense of the word. However, in practical play we often meet with positions in which a player goes in for a sacrifice without being able to calculate all its consequences.

About thirty years ago one of the leading Grandmasters of his time, Rudolf Spielmann, a keen combinative player, wrote a book called *The Art of Sacrifice in Chess.* In this book the author dealt with many of the problems connected with sacrifices on the basis of his wide personal experience. Spielmann called the sacrifices we are going to analyze real sacrifices, emphasizing that they are not of a temporary nature susceptible to accurate analysis. I cannot agree with Spielmann's classification of sacrifices as he liquidates, in effect, a concept of sacrifice which has become firmly established in chess literature all over the world, although it must be admitted that this concept needs to be more refined.

However the superb material to be found in the games of this fine player deserves thorough study and Spielmann's book can be wholeheartedly recommended to players beyond the beginner's stage. One must not draw sharp distinction between a combination and a sacrifice in the proper sense of the word. It often happens that by means of subsequent deep analysis one can establish that the maker of the sacrifice would have gained an advantage in all variations; the sacrifice could more properly be called a combination. Despite this, however, from a practical point of view, from the point of view of the struggle taking place over the board, we ought not to regard such sacrifices as combinations.

Let us start our account of sacrifices with a typical example which stands at the boundary between a combination and a sacrifice in the full sense.

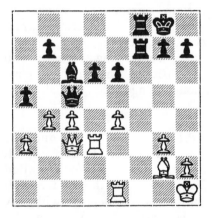

(Diagram No. 90. Rubinstein vs Spielmann, San Sebastian 1912. Black to move)

1 ...   Bxe4!

In his book Spielmann writes "The crowning point of this complicated sacrifice lies in the fact that by giving up a whole rook (the author has in mind the position occurring three moves on) the hostile king is forced into the open...*I could not calculate the combination more exactly* (we emphasize this point and certain others which follow - I. B.) and I had to rely entirely on my conviction that favorable variations would occur as a matter of course, and events proved me right".

Hence, as Black could not calculate all the consequences of his sacrifice we cannot say that Black has entered on a combination. We encounter, from the point of view of principle, a new phenomenon. There is no accurate calculation, no forced maneuver accompanying the sacrifice, winning back material or leading to mate. Hence it follows that there is no combination according to our understanding of the term. There is only a sacrifice which leads in various forced variations to positions which Spielmann assessed as being in his favor despite his material deficit since the White king is forced into perilous situations. Hence, we repeat, a sacrifice as opposed to a combination is based not on exact calculation but on *assessment of the positions* to which it leads. One must stress that it is a question here not of the **static** assessment of a normal position with material equality, but of the assessment of possibilities in a position where the material balance has been disturbed. I call such an assessment a *dynamic* assessment.

In the previous chapters we stress the fact that it is essential to develop combinative vision. Now one also has to try to develop powers of correct dynamic assessment. The best way to achieve this aim is to analyze thoroughly as large a number as possible of the various sacrifices which have occurred in practical play. This task is no less important than the study of combinations for the player who aspires to reach the top in chess. Now let us return to Spielmann's sacrifice.

2 Rxe4

Obviously White could not take the queen because of mate on f1. If 2 Bxe4 then 2...Rf1ch 3 Rxf1 Rxf1ch 4 Kg2 Rg1ch 5 Kf3 Qh5ch 6 Ke3 (*If 6 Kf4 Rf1ch*) 6...Qxh2 and at this point Spielmann concludes his analysis and writes "and White, although a bishop up, is in great and probably insurmountable difficulties on account of the exposed position of his king. *It would be*

*a problem in itself to examine the position more closely
from the practical point of view* which is the only crite-
rion we are guided by in judging real sacrifices, *only a
general assessment is possible,* which in my opinion
should be in Black's favor. He who would not boldly undertake to win such a position as Black's will never go
far in the domain of the sacrifice."

I agree with Spielmann's opinion that White stands to
lose because of his exposed king position. I consider that
modern analysis is capable of proving this rigorously.
However we shall not concern ourselves here with this
side-issue although I recommend such a thorough analysis to the reader as a very useful exercise. The main
point though is that *during the game*, Black went in for
the whole line starting 1...Bxe4 without exact calculation, as is clear from the above variation and
Spielmann's remarks. Hence, as we stress yet again, we
are not dealing with a combination as we have defined
it, but with a sacrifice which calls for the appropriate
dynamic assessment of the position. At the same time, by
proving an objective advantage for Black by forced
variations in a special analysis, we would have from the
theoretical point of view a combination. That is why this
particular example is at the boundary between combination and sacrifice.

Apart from 2 Rxe4, White has another defense in the
curious move 2 Rf3. After 2...axb4 3 axb4, Spielmann
analyzes 3...Qc6 4 b5 (*If 4 Rxe4 Qxe4 5 Rxf7 Qb1ch, etc*)
4...Rxf3 5 Qxf3! (*The best answer to the threat
5...Rf1ch*) 5...Bxf3 6 bxc6 Bxg2ch 7 Kxg2 bxc6 8
Rxe6 Rf6 9 Re7 with some drawing chances. Aside
from 3...Qc6 Black could play 3...Qh5 with a clear advantage.

2	...	Rf1ch
3	Bxf1	Rxf1ch
4	Kg2	Qf2ch
5	Kh3	

It is interesting to note that Spielmann writes "The
combination had been calculated up to this point." We
must repeat yet again that there was no combination ac-

cording to our understanding. There was merely an exact analysis of this simple variation of the sacrifice up to this point, and Black assessed the position in his favor, relying on his sense of position. White's material advantage, a whole rook, cannot save him.

5 ...   Rh1!

Black's main threat is 6...Rxh2 7 Kg4 Qf5 mate. Apart from that White has to reckon with another mate threat by 6...Qf5ch 7 Rg4 Qf1ch 8 Kh4 Rxh2ch 9 Kg5 h6ch 10 Kg6 Qf7 mate.

6 Rf3   Qxh2ch
7 Kg4   Qh5ch
8 Kf4   Qh6ch
9 Kg4   g5

White is now forced to give back a rook because of the threat 10...Qh5 mate.

10 Rxe6   Qxe6ch
11 Rf5

11 Kxg5 also loses. We suggest that the reader should confirm this by his own analysis. After the text move Black wins by 11...Qe4ch 12 Kxg5 h6ch 13 Kf6 (13 Kg6 Qg4ch) 13...Re1 14 Kg6 Qg4ch, etc.

In concluding our examination of this example we must note that in the two main variations beginning 2 Bxe4 or 2 Rxe4 (as in the game) Black's pieces maintained great activity the whole time as is very obvious. This activity persisted too in those positions which were subjected to a final assessment from the dynamic point of view. However such clearly noticeable activity of one's pieces after a sacrifice is not an essential condition. If in those variations which we considered the Black pieces had a "kinetic" energy in the final positions, so to speak, it is also possible to come across positions in which the active side, as a result of a sacrifice, has pieces which have only a "potential" energy which in the further course of play can be transformed into clearly perceptible activity. In speaking of kinetic and potential energy I am of course only drawing an analogy so as to express my ideas more clearly.

Let us examine the following position.

Tal unexpectedly made the following sacrifice which he had foreseen several moves earlier.

(Diagram No. 91. Bobotsov vs Tal, World Students' Ch 1958. Black to move)

1 ...	N x d 5
2 Qxa5	N x e 3
3 Rc1	N x c 4

A position has arisen for which Black was aiming when he sacrificed his queen for knight, bishop and pawn. Is it possible to say that in this position Black's pieces have greater "kinetic" energy? No, in my opinion, one cannot say this. At the present moment only the B g 7 exerts pressure on White's position and the knight is very well placed at c4. But Black has as yet no direct attack. Hence one could say, by way of analogy, that Black has compensation in the "potential" energy of his pieces.

Did Tal analyze the queen sacrifice? No, he went in for it only because his dynamic assessment of the position led him to it. He considered that Black's chances would not be the worse, as he himself said after the game.

It is a difficult task to assess such sacrifices correctly. Apart from purely objective difficulties, a sacrifice which violently alters the course of the game exerts (as is confirmed by experience) a definite psychological pressure on the opponent.

Very often the player who enjoys material advantage after the sacrifice strives to realize it in the belief that he has the advantage. However if the sacrifice is correct then attempts to prove it incorrect merely lead to the conception and execution of a wrong plan; disappointment may set in, and the position deteriorate.

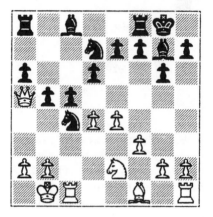

(Diagram No. 92. White to move)

We recommend the reader to analyze very carefully the position in Diagram No. 92, as well as subsequent examples arising out of sacrifices. This analysis is best done not by oneself but together with a friend which as a rule renders the analysis more objective and better develops the ability to assess hidden possibilities in the position.

After Tal's 3...Nxc4 Bobotsov decided to give up the exchange by 4 Rxc4 bxc4 5 Nc1. However Tal was able to seize the initiative after this and, developing an attack on the king along the b-file, won the game. There followed 5...Rb8 6 Bxc4 Nb6 7 Bb3 Bxd4 8 Qd2 Bg7 9 Ne2 c4 10 Bc2 c3! 11 Qd3 cxb2 12 Nd4 Bd7 13 Rd1 Rfc8 14 Bb3 Na4 15 Bxa4 Bxa4 16 Nb3 Rc3 17 Qxa6 Bxb3 18 axb3 Rbc8 and White soon resigned.

In the following classical example the psychological factor we have just mentioned played a significant part.

The sacrifice which the ex-world champion made here created a sensation at the time.

(Diagram No. 93. Ilyin-Zhenevsky vs Lasker, Moscow
1925. Black to move)

1 ...   Qxa2

"An original combination on Lasker's part" wrote
Bogolubov in the tournament book. Of course this is not
a combination.

2 Ra1   Qxb2
3 Rfb1   Qxb1ch
4 Rxb1

(Diagram No. 94. Black to move)

This is the position Lasker had in mind when he sacrificed his queen for rook, bishop and pawn. Apparently

he considered that his firm position, his good center and the possession of the two bishops would fully compensate "potentially" for his slight material deficit. On top of that he doubtless judged that the sacrifice would have a definite psychological effect on his opponent, the sort of effect we have mentioned. The subsequent course of the game confirmed the validity of these views, and Lasker won the game by fine play.

Nowadays the sacrifice of a queen for rook, minor piece and pawn turns up quite frequently. Here is another example.

(Diagram No. 95. Keres vs. Fischer, Candidates' tournament, 1959. White to move)

1 Bxf6

This exchange is the introduction to the sacrifice which follows.

1 ... Nxf6

If 1...gxf6 White gets a positional advantage by **2 f5.** 1...Bxf6 would also be met by **2 e5** as if then 2...dxe5 or 2...Bb7 White could gain an advantage by a combination beginning **3 Ndxb5!**

2 e5 Bb7

3 exf6

A combination or a sacrifice? We shall soon see.

3 ... Bxf3

4 Bxf3 Bxf6

If the **R a 8** moved away from attack White would finish up with three minor pieces against the queen with a good position by 4...Rc8 5 fxe7 Qxe7 6 Nf5!

      5 Bxa8   **d 5**
      6 Bxd5

Otherwise Black castles.

      6 ...   **B x d 4**

6...**Q x f 4 c h** is not good because of **7 Kb1 Bxd4 8 Bc6ch, 9 Ne2** and **10 Nxd4.**

      7 Rxd4   **e x d 5**
      8 Nxd5   **Q c 5**
      9 Re1ch   **K f 8**

The forced moves are over but White has not won back the material he sacrificed. There was a forced maneuver, there was a sacrifice but there is no objective advantage in the final position for the player who began the active operation. This is a sacrifice, not a combination.

(Diagram No. 96. White to move)

Keres probably thought that in the final position the bad position of Black's king and rook was a suitable prerequisite for active play by White, fully compensating the slight material deficit. It seems that Keres was right in his assessment, but in the further course of the game he played riskily and lost. (*The game continued   10 c3 h5 and now   11 f5? Various commentators gave 11 Re5! instead when White would not have had the worst of it-*

(Diagram No. 97. Petrosian vs Pfeiffer, Leipzig 1960.
White to move)

When the great positional player   Tigran Petrosian
plays a true sacrifice, it's <u>news</u>. Black's king has lin-
gered in the center - often a signal for vigorous tactics.
By a centralized piece sacrifice White gains an irre-
sistible pawn roller backed up by the excellent activity
of all White's remaining pieces.

1 Nd5!!   exd5

After 1...Qc6 2 Nf6ch! Bxf6 3 Bf3 Qa4 (3...Qc7 4
exf6 leaves Black fatally weak on the dark squares) 4
Qxa4 Nxa4 5 Bxb7 Nxb2 6 Bc6ch! Kf8 7 Rd7 Rc8 8
exf6 and White has an overwhelming position with a
rook on the 7th and mating threats due to the shocking
effect of the f6 pawn (*8...Rxc6 9 Rd8 mate; or 8...Nxc4 9
R1d1 threatening 10 Rd8 ch*).

2 cxd5

The formidable pawn duo on the 5th rank dominates
the position.

2 ...   Qc8

Avoiding the threatened 3 d6 and angling for 3...Qf5.

3 e6

With a discovered attack on the Rh8.

3 ...   0-0

On 3...f6 4 f5! is powerful.

4 Qc3!

Forcing the weakening ...f6.

    4 ...   **f 6**
    5 d6

The pawns rush forward with great effect.

    5 ...   **N a 4**
    6 Qxc8

Foreseeing that even without queens the initiative will be firmly in White's hands.

    6 ...   **R f x c 8**

Not 6...Raxc8 because 7 dxe7 hits the Rf8.

    7 Ba1

A cool retreat - a further illustration of the power of the advanced pawn duo which has now "jumped" from the 5th to the 6th rank.

    7 ...   **R c 2**

An attempt at counterattack.

    8 dxe7

Now the e7 pawn poses threats of queening.

    8 ...   **R x e 2**
    9 R d 8 c h   **K g 7**

Note how the "other" pawn at e 6 prevents the desirable ...Kf7.

    10 Rc1!

Clearing a flight square at f1 for the king and preparing to invade the 7th rank.

    10 ...   **R x e 6**

White threatened 11 Rxa8 and 12 e8=Q so the text is forced.

    11 Rc7

Seizing the 7th rank with the threat of 12 e8=Q dis. c h .

    11 ...   **K h 6**
    12 Bxf6!

A neat resource - the R e 6 is overworked having to defend both e8 and f6.

    12 ...   **B e 4**
    13 B g 5 c h

And Black resigned in view of 13...Kh5 14 e8=Q! (*A line clearing tactic*) 14...Rxe8 15 h3! (*Controlling g4 and thus threatening both 16 g4 mate as well as 16 Rxh7 mate - to which there is no defense*).

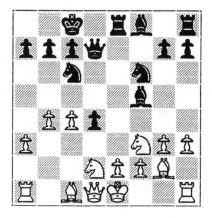

(Diagram No. 98. Bondarevsky vs Mikenas, XVIII USSR
Ch 1950. White to move)

White cannot castle as his 'h' pawn would then fall.
On the other hand, Black is pressing along the king's
file and threatens to attack the 'e' pawn by ...Bd3.
White's next move looks like a mistake, but is actually
preparation for the following sacrifice.

1	Bb2!	Bd3
2	0-0	Bxe2
3	Qa4	Bxf1
4	Rxf1	

(Diagram No. 99. Black to move)

This is the the position White had in mind when he sacrificed the exchange. Comparing Diagrams 98 and 99 the conclusion is readily reached that White has gone in for a sacrifice in order to complete his development whilst Black will still have to play for a move or so without his **Rh8**. Moreover White's king bishop exerts strong pressure on the Black game, White's queen is actively placed and the queenside pawns are ready to support an attack on the enemy king. The subsequent course of the game confirmed the correctness of White's assessment that the sacrifice was advantageous to him: **4...Kb8 5 b5 Nd8 6 Nxd4 Bc5 7 N2b3 Bxd4 8 Bxd4 b6 9 c5 Re7 10 cxb6 cxb6 11 Bxb6! axb6 12 Qa8ch Kc7 13 Qa7ch Kd6 14 Qxb6ch**, etc.

(Diagram No. 100. Miles vs Belyavsky, Tilburg 1986.
White to move)

White's **Nf5** is under fire, so it would seem that **e3-e4** is in order. But Miles finds a dynamic sacrificial continuation, taking advantage of Black's uncastled king and backward development.

1 f4!!

Damn the torpedoes, full speed ahead!

1 ...   Qxf5

If **1...Bxf5** then **2 e4** forces the **Bf5** to move after which **3 exf5** follows with crushing effect. The opening up of lines combined with White's horde of center pawns place Black's king in a critical bind. Another line is 1...gxf3 2 Rxf3 Bxf5 3 Rxf5 Qg7 4 Bxe5! (*Again, the major theme in this and similar positions is to blast open lines*) 4...dxe5 5 d6! Nc6 (*Not 5...cxd6 6 Qd5 while 5...Nd7 fails to 6 Qd5 Rc8 7 Qe6ch Kd8 8 Rf7*) 6 Qd5 Qd7 (*Of course not 6...Kd7 7 Rf7ch*) 7 Rxe5ch! Nxe5 8 Qxe5ch Kf7 9 Rf1ch Kg8 10 Rf6! (*Threatening 11 Qg3ch and if 11...Qg7 then 12 Rg6 while 11...Kh7 allows 12 Qg6 mate*) and Black will lose.

2 e4

Gaining time for the demolition of Black's position.

2 ...   Qh5
3 fxe5

Open lines!

3 ...   dxe5

Otherwise 4 exd6 or even 4 e6 is destructive.

4 c5!

Now if 4...bxc5 5 Qb5ch is strong - e.g. 5...Nd7 6 Rf5 Qg6 7 h5! Qb6 8 Rxe5ch Kf7 9 Rf1ch Kg8 10 Re8ch Kg7 11 Re7ch Kg8 12 Be5!! Qxb5 13 Rg7 mate.

4 ...   Kd8

Rather hopeless but a good defensive plan cannot be found.

5 d6!

More open lines.

5 ...   Qe8
6 dxc7 dis dbl ch   Kxc7
7 Qd5   Nc6

Forced, otherwise 8 Bxe5ch wins.

8 Rf7ch

White's rooks now pour into Black's porous defenses.

8 ...   Bd7

Not 8...Kb8 9 Qd6 mate.

9 Raf1!

Bringing up the reserves, a characteristic technique in such positions.

9 ...   Rd8
10 R1f6

Threatening 11 Qxc6ch.

10 ...   Kc8
11 cxb6   axb6
12 Qb5

And Black gave up. There is no defense to **13 Qxb6** and **14 Rxc6ch** (*14...Bxc6 15 Rc7 or Qc7 mate*). If **12...Kc7** simply **13 Rxc6ch.**

In the examples we have been examining the sacrifices were made basically for attacking purposes. The following case shows how important a sacrifice for defense can be. In such cases the psychological factor plays a big part.

(Diagram No. 101. Lyublinsky vs Botvinnik, Moscow 1943. Black to move)

Black's game is difficult as his queenside pawns are broken up and he has no compensation for this. The pawn on **c5** is particularly weak and can be attacked by three pieces (**Na4, Be3, Qf2**). Therefore Black makes a correct decision: he sacrifices the exchange, sharply changing the course of the game. Such a turn-around was probably very unpleasant for White. Obviously he would have preferred to win the forward 'c' pawn and then set about realizing his material advantage in a quiet position where his opponent had no counterplay. Now, after the exchange sacrifice, a complicated position is created which demands from White not the technical play which he was looking forward to, but deep and exact defense, as Black's counter-chances are certainly not to be underestimated.

1 ...   Rd4!

2 Ne2

White does not take the exchange at once, as he apparently did not wish to give up his second bishop, leaving his opponent with two; but as the position is rather blocked, the knight may be a better piece than the bishop. Hence a plan worthy of consideration was **2 Bxd4** followed by transferring the knight to **d3**.

2 ...   B c 8

Black could get rid of one of his weak pawns by 2...Rxd1ch 3 Rxd1 a4, as 4 bxa4 is not good for White in view of 4...Rb4. But after **4 Nc3 axb3 5 axb3** White would still have the advantage because of the weakness of the pawn on Black's **c5**. So Black still prefers to sacrifice the exchange.

3 Nxd4

As we have already pointed out, it would have been better to keep the knight and play **3 Bxd4**.

3 ...   c x d 4
4 Bf2   c 5

(Diagram No. 102. White to move)

Here are the results of White's choice of continuation: Black's position is quite firm and he has the option of attacking on the kingside by ...f5 and so on. White on the other hand finds it hard to hit upon a plan to exploit his material advantage. It is interesting to note that without making a single obvious mistake Lyublinsky gradually came under attack on the kingside and lost the game. The reason for his defeat, in my opinion, lies not only in his failure to find the right moves from the playing point of view, but also in the difficulties of re-adjusting his ideas once the game had veered sharply away from the previous run of play.

Apart from the psychological factor, it is important in practice to assess the position after a sacrifice correctly and to choose the objectively sound plan. For this pur-pose let us turn to the following example.

(Diagram No. 103. Capablanca vs Janowsky, Havana 1913.
Black to move)

Comparing this position with the one in the previous game after **1...Rd4** we can say that in this case Black has even more prospects as his strong central knight exerts great pressure on White's game. I quote this posi-tion not for a simple comparison, but to investigate how Capablanca assessed it. It is universally recognized that Capablanca had exceptional ability in assessing posi-tions of the most diverse nature. That is why his opinion is so important.

1 ...   **R b 8**

Capablanca in his book *Chess Fundamentals* writes "This move is made in order to play **Bb7** without block-ing his rook. Black's maneuvering for positional advan-tage is admirable throughout the game, and if he loses, it is entirely due to the fact that the sacrifice of the exchange did not succeed against sound defensive play."

2	Nf3	f 5
3	exf5	g x f 5

"The position begins to look really dangerous for White. In reality Black's attack is reaching its maximum. Very soon it will reach the apex and then White who is well prepared will begin his counter action and through his material superiority obtain an undoubted advantage."

4	Nf1	f 4
5	Nxd4	c x d 4

We have a position similar to the one which would have occurred in the Lyublinsky-Botvinnik game if White had captured the rook with his bishop instead of his knight.

6	Qh5	B b 7
7	Re1	c 5

"He could not play 7...Re8 because of **8 Rxd4.** Besides he wants to be ready to play ...e4. At present White cannot safely play **Rxe5,** but he will soon prepare the way for it. Then by giving up rook for bishop and pawn he will completely upset Black's attack and come out a pawn ahead. It is on this basis that White's whole defensive maneuver is founded."

8	f 3	R e 8
9	R d e 2	R e 6

"Now the rook enters the game, but White is ready for it. It is time to give back the exchange."

10	R x e 5	B x e 5
11	Rxe5	R h 6
12	Qe8	

And after accurate play in the ending, Capablanca finally won.

In practical play there are cases, admittedly rare, where the exchange is sacrificed twice over.
(See Diagram No. 104)
Black's 'h' pawn is en prise. It would not be good to defend it by **1...g6** as the king's side would be weakened and White could proceed to play **2 e4,** making progress in the center, with advantage. Black could play **1...Ng6** but here, too, after **2 Qg5** White has the better position.

Ragozin preferred to sacrifice the exchange, seizing the initiative and changing the whole course of the game.

(Diagram No. 104. Lilienthal vs Ragozin, Moscow 1935.
Black to move)

1	...	R x e 3
2	Bxe3	R x e 3
3	Nxh5	N x h 5
4	Qxh5	B c 6

In defending his 'd' pawn, Black threatens to take the 'c' pawn.

5 Qg5

5 Ra3 would be bad because of 5...Re1ch 6 Kh2 Qc7ch 7 g3 Qe7 on the rook and on the square e 2 where mate is threatened.

	5 ...	R x c 3 !

As we shall see, this leads to a second exchange sacrifice, which is what Black had in mind when he played his first move. If instead Black had played 5...Re2 then after 6 Qg3 threatening 7 Bh7ch White's position would be better, thanks to his material advantage.

6 Qd2	R x c 2

Obviously he cannot play 6...b4 because of 7 Qxc3.

7 Rxc2	N e 6

(See Diagram No. 105)

So Black has sacrificed two exchanges for a pawn. Thanks to his two united passed pawns he does not stand any the worse. White's defense is difficult and in the game Lilienthal lost as he was unable to activate his rooks.

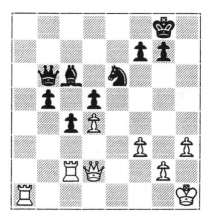

(Diagram No. 105. White to move)

There followed **8 Rd1 b4 9 Rb2 b3 10 Qc3 Nc7 11 Rbe2 Qa7 12 Qb4 Nb5 13 Re7 Qa3 14 Qe1! c3! 15 Re8ch Bxe8 16 Qxe8ch Kh7 17 Qxf7 Qa8** and Black won.

From my own games comes an occasion when, having sacrificed the exchange twice, for two pawns, I refused a draw.

(Diagram No. 106. Dely vs Bondarevsky, Budapest 1959. White to move)

In my opinion this position must be assessed as favorable to Black, as here too White has no means of actively using his rooks.

Let us examine one more sacrifice.

(Diagram No. 107. Smyslov vs Kotov, Moscow 1943. White to move)

1	Nf5!	g x f 5
2	gxf5	N c 7

2...N g 5 would be bad because of **3 Bxg5 fxg5 4 N x g 5 c h** and **5 Ne6**.

3 Rg1 etc.

The game continued 3...Ne8 4 Rg6 Rf7 5 R1g1 Kg8 6 Rxh6 Kf8 7 Rh7 Ke7 8 Qh5 Kd6 9 Bf4ch Ne5 10 Bxe5ch fxe5 11 f6! Nxf6 12 Qxe5ch Kc6 13 R7xg7! and White won.

White won although on move 3 he had only a pawn for the piece. Smyslov wrote about his first move "A typical piece sacrifice in such positions. Its special feature in this case is White's attempt *not to win back the sacrificed material* (my italics I. B) but to get an attack by systematically increasing pressure. There is no necessity here to calculate concrete variations *but I rely upon a general assessment of the position* (my italics - I.B.).

Every player who has familiarized himself with the

above examples must draw the right conclusion about the great importance of studying positions in which the material balance has been upset by a sacrifice. Once again I can recommend the compilation of a scrap-book of various sacrifices that occur in practical play.

I welcome readers' comments and requests, which will certainly be of great assistance in the preparation of a definitive work on the theory of combinations and sacrifices.

NOTES

NOTES

NOTES